D. Caroline Coile, Ph.D.

Jack Russell Terriers

Everything about Purchase, Care,
Nutrition, Behavior, and Training

With 47 Color Photographs

Illustrations by Tana Hakanson

BARRON'S

Acknowledgments

The information contained in this book comes from a variety of sources: breeders, original research, scientific articles, veterinary journals, and a library of dog books. But by far my most heartfelt gratitude must go to my most demanding teachers, who have taught me the skills of both home repair and dog repair, allowed ample testing opportunities for behavioral problem cures, and whetted my curiosity (and carpets) about everything canine for the past 20 years: Baha, Khyber, Tundra, Kara, Hypatia, Savannah, Sissy, Dixie, Bobby, Kitty, Jeepers, Bean-Boy, Junior, Khyzi, Wolfman, Stinky, Honey, and Luna.

All inquiries should be addressed to:
Barron's Educational Series, Inc.
250 Wireless Boulevard
Hauppauge, NY 11788

International Standard Book No. 0-8120-9677-0

Library of Congress Catalog Card No. 96-21777

Library of Congress Cataloging-in-Publication Data
Coile, D. Caroline.
    Jack Russell terriers : everything about adoption, purchase, care, nutrition, behavior, and training / D. Caroline Coile.
        p.   cm. — (A complete pet owner's manual)
    Includes bibliographical references (p.   ) and index.
    ISBN 0-8120-9677-0
    1. Jack Russell terrier. I. Title. II. Series.
SF429.J27C65   1996
636.7′55—dc20   96-21777
                                                    CIP

Printed in Hong Kong

98765

About the Author

Caroline Coile is an award-winning author who has written articles about dogs for both scientific and lay publications. She holds a Ph.D. in the field of neuroscience and behavior, with special interests in canine sensory systems, genetics, and behavior. A sighthound owner since 1963, her own dogs have been nationally ranked in conformation, obedience, and field-trial competition.

Photo Credits

Barbara Augello: inside front cover, pages 8 bottom, 20, 101; Melissa Nunnink-Berg: pages 29 top, 76; Susan Green: pages 32 top, 40, 65; Dale Jackson: page 96 top and bottom; Photography by O'Neill's: pages 9 top and bottom, 25 bottom; Pets by Paulette: inside back cover, pages 21, 28; Sherry Smith: front cover, pages 16, 24, 25 top, 37, 45, 48, 57, 84, 85, 89, 97; Christine Steimer: pages 8 top, 17, 29 bottom, 33, 36, 49, 60, 69, 77, 88, 93, 104; Susan Tolleson: back cover, pages 4, 32 bottom, 44, 64, 68; Jean Wentworth: pages 13, 53, 92; Elizabeth and Douglas Williams: page 12.

Important Note

This pet owner's guide tells the reader how to buy or adopt, and care for a Jack Russell terrier. The author and the publisher consider it important to point out that the advice given in the book is meant primarily for normally developed dogs of excellent physical health and good character.

Anyone who adopts a fully grown dog should be aware that the animal has already formed its basic impressions of human beings. The new owner should watch the animal carefully, including its behavior toward humans, and should meet the previous owner.

If the dog comes from a shelter, it may be possible to get some information on the dog's background and peculiarities there. There are dogs that, as a result of bad experiences with humans, behave in an unnatural manner or may even bite. Only people that have experience with dogs should take in such animals.

Caution is further advised in the association of children with dogs, in meeting with other dogs, and in exercising the dog without a leash.

Even well-behaved and carefully supervised dogs sometimes do damage to someone else's property or cause accidents. It is therefore in the owner's interest to be adequately insured against such eventualities, and we strongly urge all dog owners to purchase a liability policy that covers their dog.

Contents

Wild thing!

Preface

Scene stealer of stage shows and horse shows, too cute, too smart, and far too appealing for its own good, to see a Jack Russell terrier is to want one. And therein lies the problem. Because, for all of its appeal as an irascible fun-loving scamp, the Jack Russell terrier (JRT) was born to hunt. These dogs seek out trouble. That's part of their appeal, but also part of the difficulty of owning them.

More popular at horse shows than dog shows, the Jack Russell terrier is the most popular "rare" breed in America. Since it is totally ignored by most dog books and excluded from AKC recognition, one might think that JRT owners would be angered by this apparent snub. But, in fact, JRT owners traditionally guard their secret breed jealously, avoiding AKC recognition and discouraging over-popularity. Yet this attitude of exclusivity has its price—the lack of information readily available to the average JRT owner.

This book is intended to fill that gap, and to provide both prospective and current JRT owners with information specific to this most versatile of dogs. If you decide you are ready to take a walk on the wild side, begin your adventure with the best JRT companion out there. Finding a good JRT entails special challenges, and the tips contained in this book will help you avoid the many pitfalls involved. Add to this advice on JRT health, grooming, training, feeding, breeding, and enjoying, and you should be ready to begin the adventure of a lifetime.

Note: Jack Russells come in a wide variety of types, not all of which are correct according to the standards. They do, however, represent the many faces of the Jack Russell terrier, and as such, may be included among the photos in this book. The reader is cautioned, however, that extremely short-legged JRTs are not considered desirable from a functional and traditional viewpoint.

The JRT is at the center of a heated debate concerning the pros and cons of AKC recognition, as well as the definition of true Jack Russell type. The intent of this book is not to advocate one position over another, but to present both viewpoints so that the reader can help make an informed decision about the future of the Jack Russell terrier.

What Makes Jack Russell Terriers So Different?

To understand the Jack Russell terrier you must accept one fact: This is a dog driven by an overpowering instinctive urge to hunt. To understand why this urge is so well developed in today's Jack Russells, you must delve into the story of the Jack Russells of yesterday.

Jack Russell Had a Dog

Many breeds have an ancient and mysterious origin—the Jack Russell terrier is not one of them. The Jack Russell terrier (JRT) originated in large part from the descendants of a terrier bitch named "Trump," and were selectively bred in the mid- to late

A dog bred to run wherever a fox runs, the JRT is understandably built much like a fox.

1800s by a clergyman in Devonshire, England named John Russell. Like so many of his countrymen, the Reverend John Russell had a passion for fox hunting, and many strains of fox terrier-type dogs were in use at the time for bolting or even dispatching foxes. But the strain developed by John Russell proved itself to be exceptionally rugged and game and quickly made a name for itself—indeed, it took the name of its founder, the Parson John (Jack) Russell.

John Russell's interest in dogs led him also to become one of the founders of England's Kennel Club, perhaps the most influential dog registration body in the world, and the organization most responsible for the sport of showing purebred dogs in conformation competitions. In fact, John Russell judged fox terriers at the very first Kennel Club dog show. Yet, it is a curious fact that John Russell never once exhibited his own Jack Russell terriers at a conformation show. Did John Russell foresee a problem that the proponents of other breeds may have only recognized too late?

No doubt John Russell would have difficulty recognizing the fox terriers trotting around today's show rings. The modern fox terrier has been exaggerated, beautified, and "improved" to the point that, while it is a stunning and highly competitive show dog, it bears little resemblance to the working fox terrier that was its foundation. The premise of dog shows—the idea that a dog's working ability could be evaluated on the basis of its structure alone—had failed to take into consideration human nature. The desire to outdo the competition inevitably leads to selection for extremes and exaggeration, all too often without regard for function, and all too often resulting in a breed that can no longer perform its original job. Perhaps John Russell understood human nature a little more than did his fellow breeders, or perhaps he simply found the hunt far more exhilarating than a day spent in the show benching area. Whatever the reason, he declined to show his dogs and in so doing, perhaps had his most lasting influence upon the breed that bears his name.

Tradition

Advocates of the Jack Russell terrier followed John Russell's example, proving their dogs in the field rather than in the ring—much to these fun-loving dog's delight! The tradition has remained intact now for well over a century. This emphasis upon field ability over conformation aspects is at the heart of what makes a Jack Russell terrier different from most other breeds of dog.

Not only do JRT proponents traditionally reject the idea of showing their dogs, but they have also traditionally been vehemently opposed to official recognition of their breed by multi-breed dog registration bodies such as the Kennel Club in England or the American Kennel Club in the United States. They are opposed not only because of the emphasis these organizations place upon conformation dog shows, but also because these are purely pedigree-based registries. Any dog whose parents are registered with that organization is itself eligible for registration, and thus subsequent

Still very much at home around the stables, Jack Russells are the breed of choice among many horse people.

breeding, no matter what the quality of that individual dog is. But, as the JRT is first and foremost a working terrier, its advocates consider evidence of pure breeding to be secondary to hunting ability and good health.

The Jack Russell terrier has been called "the most popular mutt in the world," referencing its frequent crosses to a smorgasbord of terrier breeds. This, coupled with the practice of interbreeding with exceptional hunting JRTs often lacking proof of pure JRT breeding, cause many people to call JRTs a strain, rather than a breed, of dog. Again, the emphasis upon ability

"You mean you didn't want a hole here?" When it comes to digging, JRTs are doers, not talkers.

Born to hunt.

over looks has led to a strain that varies considerably in type and size from dog to dog, a situation that creates some consternation among judges at conformation shows. The JRT is not a cookie-cutter breed!

JRTs come in different coat types, body sizes, and leg lengths, with height being a point of contention among many present-day breeders. The JRT was originally bred not to kill the fox, but to cause it to bolt from any hiding place so that the fox hunt could continue. Thus it had to be fast enough to run with the hounds, small enough to squeeze into a burrow, plucky enough to face a snarling fox at close range, and ferocious enough to scare the fox out. Its job was to bark at the fox, not kill it.

In the early 1900s, the British countryside became crossed with barbed wire fencing, aiding the decline of riding to the hounds. A new type of fox hunter emerged who wanted a dog that would be an ally to a man on foot. Thus, a shorter-legged, slower, but scrappier, terrier, whose job was to actually dispatch the fox, was favored, and the JRT was interbred with such dogs. The tough, short-legged result was also an excellent ratter and badger hunter, activities more readily accessible to the common man. But was it really a Jack Russell terrier?

The stage was set for a heated debate still raging today: Which is the proper and true JRT? The traditional longer-legged dog said to be favored by the Parson himself (sometimes referred to as the Parson Jack Russell terrier), or the shorter-legged dog dominating the breed in more recent times? The debate has caused the formation of separate JRT clubs, each of which allows a different range in size and has opposing beliefs about what is best for the future of the breed.

One Goal, Two Paths

The Jack Russell Terrier Club of America (JRTCA) and the JRT Club of Great Britain have standards that allow for a wider range in height, including a shorter (but not dwarf-type) JRT. Both clubs adamantly oppose JRT recognition by any all-breed registry.

The Jack Russell Terrier Breeder's Association (JRTBA) and the Parson JRT Club in England both favor the old type longer-legged (Parson) JRT, and both encourage recognition by all-breed registries. In 1991 the English Kennel Club recognized the (British) Parson JRT; the JRTBA is currently working toward AKC recognition. Already in the United States the United Kennel Club, States Kennel Club, American Rare Breed Association, and several other smaller registries recognize JRTs. Breeders advocating recognition contend that owners should be able to choose whether or not they wish to partake in dog-showing activities, and have confidence that knowledgeable breeders will not forsake working aptitude for show ring success. The evolution of the Parson Jack Russell Terrier in England will be testimony to whether or not this confidence is well placed.

Unfortunately, this disagreement about the best way to serve the breed has created a rift among JRT supporters, and this lack of unification can only hurt the breed. The JRTCA will not accept members who register their dogs with the JRTBA or any multi-breed registry. Yet some registries, such as the United Kennel Club, sponsor obedience and agility competitions that offer a fun way for owners to interact with their dogs. The JRTCA also offers these competitions, but may not be as readily available in all parts of the country. Thus, JRT pet owners who simply want to enjoy their dogs are forced to make a decision, and to limit their areas of activity.

The Jack Russell terrier is now more popular than ever as a lively, intelligent, and attractive companion, but its first love is still for the hunt.

A familiar sight around the stables.

Members of both organizations love the breed dearly, and work diligently to ensure its future. They may disagree on the methods, but there is one thing they do agree on—the JRT must be safeguarded to preserve its health, working instinct, and temperament, and it must be cautiously promoted lest it be placed with new owners who are not prepared to deal with the rambunctious and unique nature of the breed.

Today, most JRTs find fulfilling lives serving the most important function any dog can—that of pet. The breed has enjoyed immense popularity in England for many years, and is rapidly gaining an almost cult-like following in America and elsewhere. The JRT is especially popular with the "horse set," no doubt in part because it looks right at home accompanying the well turned-out hunter. It is a popular co-star of television shows, movies, and commercials, and this exposure, combined with the dog's saucy expression, humorous antics, and intelligent nature no doubt will continue to win more people over to this pert little breed. Long-time aficionados worry, however, that with such popularity comes the danger of careless breeding, overpopulation, exploitation, and poor placement of pups. For a breed that has survived over a century virtually unchanged, there is a dangerous crossroad ahead. This breed is definitely not suited for everyone, and an incompatible match of dog and owner can spell a lifetime of shared unhappiness, or—far too often—a trip to the pound.

Too many people acquire a dog with the assumption that all breeds act the same. They do not. The very reason that different breeds were initially created stemmed from differences in behavior, not looks. Dogs were selected for their propensity to trail, point, retrieve, herd, protect, or even cuddle, with physical attributes often secondary to behavioral. More than most breeds, with its long history of selection based upon function, the JRT is a prime example. The JRT was selected to hunt by investigating, running, digging, and barking. Don't get a Jack Russell terrier and ask it to act like a lapdog. It's simply not its nature.

The Nature of the Beast

Many people look at a JRT and see an irresistibly cute dog with an impish face and they simply must have one. They see the Hollywood JRT stars and assume they are all smart, wonderful pets, but all too often new JRT owners are unprepared to deal with the JRT's never ending quest for adventure, and far too often unprepared owners lose their enthusiasm for their unmanageable pet and ultimately dispose of it. Look before you leap into JRT ownership!

Temperament

Over 100 years of selection for working ability has produced a dog that loves to hunt. These dogs need to be bold, energetic, inquisitive, and relentless. Because the JRT's hunting style is not based upon following the hunter's directions (as it is in many sporting breeds, for example), they need to be independent and self-directed. They must be tough and tenacious in the face of adversity (even if that adversity is their owner telling them *"No!"*). They must be untiring in order to follow the fox over great distances and keep it at bay for long periods (as any owner knows who has ever tried to catch a runaway JRT). They must bark with vigor and stamina (much to the next door neighbor's dismay). They must be willing, indeed, anxious, to seek out quarry and follow it underground. Allowed to roam the neighborhood, the JRT feels compelled to range far afield and may not return for days, or at all; in fact, some JRTs have been found ensconced underground after days, unwilling to leave their quarry at any cost. Left alone in the yard, they will dig in search of buried treasure.

Everyone wants an intelligent dog, but few people realize that it is often much easier to live with a dumb dog than a smart one, especially when that intelligence is combined with independence. The JRT is an intelligent, independent dog.

JRTs tend to be leaders, and should be obedience-trained so that they accept you as leader. Give a JRT an inch, and it will likely take several miles. This doesn't mean it needs to be "shown who's boss" with force—just a consistent gentle but firm hand.

Getting Along with Other Animals

Most terriers are not good candidates for "Miss Congeniality Awards" when it comes to getting along with other dogs, but JRTs are somewhat the exception. Because they were meant to run with other dogs while hunting, the proper JRT should get along well with them. But not all JRTs have this proper outlook, and the fact that many have been crossed with less amiable terriers in the quest for a JRT that could actually kill the fox (a fellow canid) has resulted in some JRTs that are not compatible with other dogs. Nor are they good with hamsters, gerbils, ferrets, and cats, unless raised with them or otherwise carefully trained and supervised.

Breeders have been extremely successful in producing a dog that fits the bill when it comes to bolting and dispatching foxes and small mammals, and the JRT is very likely the best hunting terrier in the world. If you want a hunting terrier, look no further—this is your breed. But if you want a quiet lapdog, keep on looking!

Exercise Is Essential

This is not to say that the JRT cannot make a great pet—indeed, just the contrary! But it absolutely must have the chance to exercise both its body and mind with daily outdoor activity; otherwise, it is likely to exercise both by creating special effects on your home with its teeth and nails. Owners who want a JRT primarily as a pet must commit themselves to changing their lifestyles to fit that of the JRT, because compromise is not in this breed's vocabulary!

Catch of the day: Two Jack Russells that define tenacity.

Although JRTs require an inordinate amount of exercise, they can derive as much joy from killing toys in your living room as they could rats in the field. They will provide their owners with hours of entertainment with their robust sense of humor and clownish antics. They learn quickly, and are eager to please as long as there is some fun involved. But even JRTs must rest, and when they fall asleep at their owner's feet, the owner, too, can rest with the assurance that they are in the protective custody of an extremely loyal and fearless companion. JRTs are excellent watchdogs, and can be menacing protection dogs. They can make fun-loving friends for children, too, but they will not put up with any abusive treatment. They are not the breed of choice for very young children who may not realize that they are being rough. The JRT is a dog used to fending for itself, and is liable to nip in response to such rough treatment.

And remember, JRTs sleep. But not very often.

Health

Aside from the temperament traits needed to be a good hunting JRT, there are certain physical features that are common to typical Jack Russell terriers. One is good health. Many popular purebreeds are plagued by hereditary health problems, but Jack Russell terriers are affected by very few such problems.

• *Lens luxation,* wherein the lens of one or (more commonly) both eyes becomes displaced, is the most prevalent hereditary disorder in the breed, yet it is still uncommon. Left untreated, the condition can result in secondary glaucoma and lead to loss of vision. This condition is believed to have a genetic basis, in part because it is more widespread in the terrier breeds than in any others; in fact, one researcher in England has reported seeing more cases in JRTs than in any other breed. This is not to imply that the breed is swamped with luxated lenses; however, it is a condition about which breeders should be wary.

• *Primary glaucoma* (increased pressure within the eye), *corneal dystrophy* (opacity of the clear surface of the eye), and *progressive retinal atrophy* (PRA, deterioration of the visual receptors of the retina) have also been reported in the breed, but are not believed to be widespread.

• Also reported is *progressive neuronal abiotrophy* (PNA, or ataxia), in which dogs develop tremors and severe lack of coordination, and ultimately are unable to stand or even eat. It results from the degeneration of cells in the cerebellum, that part of the brain responsible for making smooth, coordinated movements. The condition is believed to be hereditary, but again, is not widespread.

• *Patellar luxation* has been reported, but is now less common than in previous times. It is more common in shorter-legged JRTs. In this condition the patella (kneecap) slips from the groove in front of the knee and becomes displaced to the side, rendering the dog unable to straighten the leg. Affected dogs may stand bowlegged or cow-hocked. Such dogs will hold the leg up for a few steps when moving until the patella pops back into place. The condition can be corrected surgically.

• *Legg-Calve-Perthes* disease involves deterioration of the head of the femur (thigh bone), usually of one leg. It is usually not apparent until about seven months of age, when the dog may be slightly lame. Degenerative joint disease eventually causes more severe lameness.

• *Deafness* has been reported in one (unilateral) or both (bilateral) ears. Bilaterally deaf dogs should be apparent by the time the pups are of selling age, but it is difficult to detect a unilat-

"Prepare to meet your fate, grasshopper!"

erally deaf dog. A test (brain stem auditory evoked response, or BAER) is available at most veterinary teaching hospitals that can detect hearing loss in pups as young as five weeks of age by monitoring electrical impulses in the dog's brain in response to noises.

• Some JRTs have very *short toes,* so short that the nails appear to stick straight forward. The condition seems to be caused by premature closing of the growth plate. Although such toes would not be evident in a young pup, they seem to cause no problems and are of concern only if you want your JRT for competition or breeding.

• Also sometimes found in JRTs are missing teeth, occlusion problems, allergic dermatitis, and undescended testicles—problems common to all pure breeds.

Although any hereditary disease is one too many, the above list is short in the world of purebred dogs. The abundance of skeletal, retinal, and cardiac disorders common in so many other breeds have not made their appearance in Jack Russells. With responsible breeding, let's hope the list gets shorter, not longer.

JRTs and children love to play together, but should be supervised to ensure that they treat one another with gentleness.

The number one cause of death in Jack Russell terriers is being hit by cars. Owner carelessness and blind trust are the insidious killers. Those that avoid accidents typically live to be 13 or 14 years of age, with unusual (but not rare) JRTs reaching 17 or 18 years.

Conformation

Despite the fact that JRT breeders have traditionally not emphasized conformation and rejected the idea of registration based simply upon evidence of pure breeding, it does not mean that these dogs have been bred with no guidelines. Nothing could be further from the truth. But first and foremost, the guideline has been ability in the field.

Hunting JRTs must not only be willing to follow a fox (or other quarry) to ground, but they must be physically able to do so. This ability does require certain features of conformation, most notably strong legs, a flexible torso, and a small chest. The Parson Russell described the ideal JRT conformation as that "of an adult vixen red fox, approximately 14 inches [36 cm] at the withers and 14 pounds [6.4 kg] in weight."

JRTs should be able to do the job for which they were bred with a minimum of exertion and maximum of effect, and without becoming lame in the process. This attribute is known as *soundness.* Despite the emphasis upon function, breeders of JRTs also want their dogs to look like JRTs; that is, they should possess the attribute of Jack Russell terrier *type.* Add these attributes of soundness and type to the requirements of *good health* and *temperament,* and you have the four cornerstones of the ideal Jack Russell terrier.

Several breed standards exist for the JRT. This, combined with the wide variety in size, coat, and type that is acceptable within the more popular of these standards, allows for great variation within the breed. This variability is one of the breed's attributes, allowing for specialization within the breed for hunting different quarry over different terrain. It is also the source of much disagreement, as some JRT purists believe the wide acceptance only promotes a generic terrier of questionable Jack Russell ancestry and type.

Standard Terms

withers: high point over the shoulder blades

stop: change in level between the forehead and muzzle

occiput: rearmost point of backskull

level bite: bite in which incisors meet each other rather than with the top overlapping the bottom

loin: area of the back over the abdomen

angulation: angles formed between the pelvis, stifle, and hock

stifle: knee

hock: ankle

brindle: tan color overlaid with vertical black stripes.

The original JRT standard was drafted in 1904 by the founder of the Parson Jack Russell Club, Arthur Heineman. The current JRTBA standard was modeled after the Heineman standard, and the term Parson Jack Russell terrier is sometimes used to distinguish dogs fitting the Heineman standard, as opposed to shorter-legged JRTs.

The JRTCA standard was drafted in 1975. Because it is the most popular JRT standard in the United States, it is printed here. If the AKC ever recognizes the JRT, it is likely that the JRTBA standard would become the official standard. Both standards describe the same tough and lively hunter, but with some subtle differences. These are laid out under the appropriate sections (in italics) as *JRTBA Notes*. The most important difference is that the JRTBA standard disqualifies JRTs under 12 inches (30 cm) or over 15 inches (38 cm) at the withers.

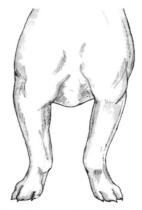

Bowed front legs are often seen on short-legged JRTs. As the signature of an achondroplastic dwarf, they are incorrect for the breed.

JRTCA Official Breed Standard

Characteristics: The terrier must present a lively, active, and alert appearance. It should impress with its fearless and happy disposition. It should be remembered that the Jack Russell is a working terrier and should retain these instincts. Nervousness, cowardice or overaggressiveness should be discouraged, and it should always appear confident.

JRTBA Note: The JRTBA standard adds that the JRT is bold, friendly, athletic, clever, tenacious, playful, exuberant, independent, and affectionate. Faults are shyness or over-aggressive behavior. A distinction is made between shyness and submissive behavior, which is not a fault.

General Appearance: A sturdy, tough terrier, very much on its toes all of the time, measuring between 10 inches and 15 inches (25–38 cm) at the withers. The body length must be in proportion to the height, and it should present a compact, balanced image, always being in solid, hard condition.

JRTBA Note: The JRTBA standard calls for both sexes to be between 12 inches and 14 inches (30–36 cm) at the withers, with mature males ideally 14 inches (36 cm), and females 13 inches (33 cm). Weight should be between 13 and 16 pounds (6–7.3 kg). Height of under 12 inches (30 cm) or over 15 inches (38 cm) is a disqualification.

Head: Should be well-balanced and in proportion to the body. The skull should be flat, of moderate width at the ears, narrowing to the eyes. There should be a defined stop but not overly pronounced. The length of muzzle from the nose to the stop should be slightly shorter than the distance from the stop to the occiput. The nose should be black. The jaw should be powerful and well boned with strongly muscled cheeks.

JRTBA Note: The JRTBA standard disqualifies a dog with liver-colored nose.

Jack Russells like to dig and burrow, especially in your bedcovers!

The incorrect short toe sticks straight out instead of arching down to the ground.

Neck: Clean and muscular, of good length, gradually widening at the shoulders.

Forequarters: The shoulders should be sloping and well laid back, fine at points, and clearly cut at the withers. Forelegs should be strong and straight-boned with joints in correct alignment. The elbows should be hanging perpendicular to the body and working free of the sides.

Body: The chest should be shallow and narrow, and the front legs set not too widely apart, giving an athletic, rather than heavily chested, appearance. As a guide only, the chest should be small enough to be easily spanned behind the shoulders, by average-size hands, when the terrier is in a fit, working, condition. The back should be strong, straight and, in comparison to the height of the terrier, give a balanced image. The loin should be slightly arched.

JRTBA Note: The JRTBA standard lists as a fault a chest that is not spannable by average-size hands, or barrel ribs. It instructs that to measure the chest, span from behind, lifting the front legs off the ground, and squeeze gently.

Hindquarters: Strong and muscular, well put together with good angulation and bend of stifle, giving plenty of drive and propulsion. Seen from behind, the hocks must be straight.

Feet: Round, hard-padded, of cat-like appearance, neither turning in or out.

JRTBA Note: The JRTBA standard lists hare-feet as a fault.

Tail: Should be set rather high, carried gaily and in proportion to body length, usually about 4 inches (10 cm) long, providing a good hand-hold.

JRTBA Note: The JRTBA standard adds that the tail is docked so that the tip is approximately level to the skull, and that the tail should be carried gaily but not over the back or curled.

Eyes: Should be almond-shaped, dark in color, and full of life and intelligence.

JRTBA Note: The JRTBA standard lists round, light, or yellow eyes as faults.

Ears: Small V-shaped drop ears carried forward close to the head and of moderate thickness.

JRTBA Note: The JRTBA standard disqualifies a dog with prick ears. Hound ears, fleshy ears, or ears with round tips are considered faults.

Mouth: Strong teeth with the top slightly overlapping the lower. (*Note:* A level bite is acceptable for registration.)

JRTBA Note: The JRTBA standard disqualifies a dog with overshot, undershot, or wry mouth, or more than four missing teeth. A level bite or any missing teeth are considered faults.

Coat: Smooth, without being so sparse as to not provide a certain amount of protection from the elements and undergrowth. Rough or broken coated, without being wooly.

JRTBA Note: The JRTBA standard requires that both coat types be double-coated, coarse, and weather-proof. Neither should have a bare belly or bare undersides of thighs. The broken coat is harsh, straight, wiry, and lies close to the body and legs. The outline is clear, with only a hint of eyebrows and beard, and no sculptured furnishings. The smooth coat is flat, but hard, dense, and abundant. All dogs should be shown in a natural appearance; excessive grooming or sculpting is to be penalized. Faults: Soft, silky, wooly, curly coat, or lack of undercoat.

Color: White should predominate (i.e., must be more than 51 percent white) with tan, black, or brown markings. Brindle markings are unacceptable.

JRTBA Note: The JRTBA standard disqualifies dogs with brindle markings. It also notes that colors should be clear, and preferably confined to the head and root of tail. Heavy body markings are not desirable.

Gait: Movement should be free, lively, and well coordinated with straight action in front and behind.

JRTBA Note: The JRTBA standard also calls for ample reach and drive with a good length of stride.

Note: For showing purposes, terriers are classified into two groups: 10 to 12½ inches (25.4–31.8 cm); and over 12½ inches and up to 15 inches.

JRTBA Note: The JRTBA disqualifies dogs under 12 inches (30.5 cm) or over 15 inches (38 cm).

Old scars or injuries, the result of work or accident, should not be allowed to prejudice a terrier's chance in the show ring unless they interfere with its movement or with its utility for work or stud.

The proper JRT is a basically square dog, with its height at the withers about the same as the length of its body.

Male animals should have two apparently normal testicles fully descended into the scrotum.

JRTBA Note: Dogs that do not have two normal testicles in the scrotum are disqualified.

A Jack Russell terrier should not show any strong characteristics of another breed.

Faults:
- shyness
- disinterest
- overaggression
- defects in bite
- weak jaws
- fleshy ears
- down at the shoulder
- barrel ribs
- out at elbow
- narrow hips
- straight stifles
- weak feet
- sluggish or unsound movement
- dishing
- plaiting
- toeing
- silky or wooly coats

- too much color (less than 51 percent white)
- shrill or weak voice
- lack of muscle or skin tone
- lack of stamina or lung reserve
- evidence of foreign blood

Requirements for Registration with the JRTCA

Dogs applying for registration must be over one year of age and be owned by a member of the JRTCA. They must present the following documents:

- *Stud service certificate* signed by the owner of the dog's sire.
- *Four generation pedigree.* Products of inbreedings (mother/son, father/daughter, brother/sister) are not acceptable, and half sister/half brother matings are allowable only once in every three generations.
- *Veterinary certificate.* Dogs must be clear of defects of possible hereditary nature, such as cryptorchidism, eye problems, bite problems, luxated patellas, and some hernias.

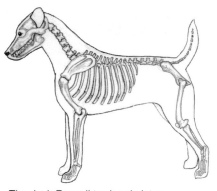

The Jack Russell terrier skeleton.

- *Color photographs.* Dogs must be evaluated from the front and both sides to ensure that they generally adhere to the breed standard. Not only must a JRT be of pure breeding, but in order to be registered it must further be evaluated based upon its own merits. Application cannot be made until the dog is one year of age, and each applicant must be approved on an individual basis and supply documentation attesting to its pure breeding, freedom from hereditary defects, and general adherence to the breed standard. The JRTCA is the largest club and registry of JRTs in the world, now with nearly 4,000 members and over 6,000 registered JRTs. The club awards several prestigious certificates based upon working abilities of JRTs, and also awards conformation titles, but only to JRTs that have already proven their mettle in the field. The JRTCA will not allow into its membership anyone who registers their JRT with any conflicting kennel club, nor who is a member of the JRTBA.

Dogs failing in some requirements may not be registered, but can still be recorded, which enables them to compete in JRTCA hunting trials. And after all, that's the most fun!

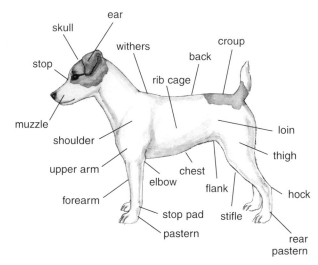

Some terms used in the Jack Russell terrier breed standard.

In Search of a Jack Russell Terrier

Your JRT-to-be should come from a reputable source that upholds the high standards with which this breed has come to be identified. Unfortunately, with increasing popularity, JRTs are found with greater frequency in backyard breeding pens. Don't encourage irresponsible breeding, and don't settle for less than the best this great breed has to offer. Your JRT will be a part of your family and life for the next 10 to 15 years. Spend the time now to make those years the best possible. This process will require a lot of decision making.

Decisions, Decisions

Puppy or Adult?

Puppies are not for everyone. No one can deny that a puppy is cute and fun, but a young puppy is much like a baby; you can't ever be too busy to walk, feed, supervise, or clean (and clean and clean). If you work away from home, have limited patience, or heirloom rugs, an older puppy or adult may be a better choice.

Young JRT pups are actually fairly obedient but when they reach adolescence at around seven months of age, all rudiments of domestication may sometimes appear to be lost! Obedience training is a necessity for both adolescents and adults if they are to live in a civilized world.

Most adult Jack Russells adjust quickly and can form new attachments in a short time. Still, older JRTs, especially kennel dogs, may have a difficult time adjusting to other pets or children.

The easiest transition time for puppies is between 8 and 12 weeks of age, but if you definitely want a competition-quality dog you may have to wait until 5 or 6 months of age. No matter what the age, if the puppy has been properly socialized (that is, treated gently and exposed to a variety of situations, people, and dogs), your JRT will soon blend into your family life and love you as though it's always owned you.

Male or Female?

Both males and females have comparably wonderful and mischievous personalities. Many breeders believe the JRT males tend to be a little more people-oriented and sweeter, and the females a little busier and hunting motivated.

The bad points:
• Females come in estrus ("season" or "heat") twice a year; this lasts for three weeks, during which time you must keep her away from amorous neighborhood males who have chosen your house as the place to be. You must also contend with her bloody discharge and possible attempts to elope with her suitors.
• Males are apt to go off in search of females, and often think nothing of repeatedly lifting their leg on your furniture to mark your house as their territory.

The solution: **neutering.** Your JRT will be better behaved, cleaner, and healthier if it is spayed or neutered at an early age.
• *Spaying* (surgical removal of ovaries and uterus) before the first season

A puppy requires the same vigilant care you would give to a human baby.

eliminates the estrous cycle and drastically reduces the chances of breast or uterine cancer.

• *Castration* (surgical removal of the testicles) virtually eliminates the chance of testicular or prostate cancer. Dogs with undescended testicles have an increased risk of testicular cancer, and should be castrated before three to five years of age.

Note: In a recent study, 80 percent of all dogs killed by automobiles were intact (unneutered) males, apparently making their rounds.

Smooth, Rough, or In-between?

JRTs come in three coat types: smooth, rough, and broken. The broken coat is intermediate between the other types, having the appearance of a short coarse coat, perhaps with slight facial furnishings. The rough coat requires regular stripping (see page 62) if it is to keep its proper JRT neat appearance. All coat types shed year round. Some JRT owners believe the smooth coat sheds more, but all hair sheds the same—the smooth hairs may just be better at weaving themselves into your clothing!

JRTCA or JRTBA Registered?

Your JRT cannot be registered with both. The JRTCA is by far the larger of the two major registration bodies. Both clubs offer a variety of activities, but because the JRTCA is larger, it has more events. The associations differ in their attitude concerning AKC and other all-breed club recognition, with the JRTCA being dead set against it. They also differ in their interpretation of the correct size and leg length of the JRT, with the JRTBA strongly advocating a longer-legged terrier. The JRTBA registers pups at birth, while the JRTCA will not register them until over a year of age. If you plan on breeding or in any way competing with your JRT, its registration body is a very important decision. Contact both clubs and see for yourself which ideals you prefer.

Short-legged or Long-legged?

The short-legged JRTs are very popular as pets, but are incorrect according to the JRT standard. In fact, most of these short-legged dogs have bowed front legs, the hallmark signature of an achondroplastic dwarf. Many such dwarf breeds exist in the dog world as a product of selective breeding, but the traditional Jack Russell terrier is not one of them. Short-legged JRTs make wonderful pets, but don't expect to register them with the JRTCA. If you want a competition-quality dog, get a long-legged Jack Russell with a square, proportioned body.

The More Terriers the Merrier?

There are certain advantages, and disadvantages, to having more than one dog. Two dogs are twice the fun of one, without being twice the work—unless they fight. Terriers are notorious for quarreling with each other, but JRTs are bred to get along with other members of a hunting pack. Still, they cannot totally shake their terrier heritage, so it is best to not get two members of the same sex.

In most families, two JRTs of the opposite sex will get along just fine; however, a third JRT may not fit in so well. It is especially not advisable to leave more than two JRTs alone and unsupervised. If you have more than two JRTs, be warned that other dogs will often jump on and attack the loser in a scuffle. Neutered dogs are less likely to fight and neutering will prevent the headache of keeping Jack and Jill separated during her seasons.

All Dogs Are Not Created Equal

One of the reasons for choosing a purebred dog is the assurance that it will look and act a certain way when it matures. JRTs come in a wide range of types, but at some point an alleged JRT no longer even resembles a JRT. Why pay purebred prices for a dog that doesn't even resemble a pure breed?

In most breeds, the term "AKC registered" is touted as a major advertising point. JRTs cannot be AKC registered, but can be registered with the JRTCA or JRTBA. Because the JRTCA registration is not automatically bestowed simply because the parents were registered, the JRTCA designation signifies that a dog not only is of pure parentage, but possesses certain minimal requirements of health and type.

Still, a key word here is *minimal.* If you want your JRT to be "just" a pet, then such minimal requirements are probably all that you will need. If, however, you want to compete with your JRT in terrier trials or other events, you will want to select a pup from parents that have themselves excelled in such endeavors.

Most of the short-legged JRTs, so popular as pets, are incorrect by either associations' standards. Proper JRT proportion is that of a square-bodied dog, equal in length and height. The short-legged terriers have their own special

You can't have just one! Jack Russell terriers can entertain each other for hours.

appeal, but don't expect to compete with them successfully at JRT events.

No matter what your plans are for your new JRT, you should try to get a puppy from parents that are both registered with one of the national JRT associations. You want to avoid a puppy from parents whose only claim to breeding quality is fertility, and you want to avoid buying from a breeder whose only claim to that title is owning a fertile dog. You may think that if you only want pet quality you don't have to be so careful, but consider the most important attributes of a pet: good health and good temperament.

Buy the best dog, with the best parents, from the best breeder possible. It is also best if you can see the parents and puppies in the flesh, and even better if you get some type of guarantee. But a word of caution about guarantees from any source: No guarantee can reimburse you for your broken heart when your puppy dies. And replacement guarantees that require you to return the original dog aren't worth much when you already love that original dog.

How Dogs Are Graded

Dogs are generally graded as pet, show (or competition), and breeding quality, although these terms are less frequently used for JRTs.

• A pet-quality dog is one that has some cosmetic fault that would prevent it from winning in a conformation ring, terrier trial, or from receiving JRTCA registration. It should still be of good health and temperament. Being a pet is the most important role a dog can fulfill, and pet quality should never be scoffed at.

• Show- or competition-quality dogs should first of all be pet quality; that is, they should have good temperament and health. In addition, they should portray the attributes called for in the breed standard, and possess the potential to excel in the field.

• With few exceptions, breeding quality dogs come from impeccable backgrounds, and are of even higher quality than are show/competition-quality dogs. Breeding quality means more than the ability to impregnate or conceive, but far too often these are the only criteria applied to prospective parents by owners unduly impressed by a registration certificate. It is difficult to pick a show-quality puppy at an early age; it is impossible to pick a breeding-quality puppy.

Choose Your Source Carefully

The better quality you demand, the longer your search will take. A couple of months is a reasonable time to spend looking for a pet puppy, a couple of years for a breeding-quality dog. Begin your search for a high-quality JRT by seeing as many JRTs as possible, talking to JRT breeders, attending JRT competitions, and reading every available JRT publication.

No matter what quality JRT you want, some sources are better than others. The best way to locate a JRT is to contact one of the JRT registries and ask for a list of breeders in your area, and for a schedule of coming events so that you can see a number of JRTs from different breeders in the flesh. *True Grit,* the JRTCA newsletter, is an excellent source for upcoming litter announcements. Another possibility is one of the all-breed dog magazines (*Dog World* or *Dogs USA*). For addresses, see Useful Addresses and Literature, page 98.

Breeders

Why contact a serious breeder if you "only" want a pet? Because these breeders will have raised your pet as though it were their next big winner. It will have received the same prenatal care, nutrition, and socialization as every prospective competition dog in that litter. The pup has the benefit of the dedicated breeder's years of study of the breed. Such breeders should be knowledgeable and conscientious enough to have also considered temperament and health when planning the breeding. If this is to be your first Jack Russell terrier, you will need continued advice from an experienced JRT owner as your puppy grows. The serious hobby breeder is just a phone call away, and will be concerned that both you and the puppy are getting along well. In fact, because many breeders will expect to keep in touch with the owners of all of the puppies throughout their lives, you may find yourself a member of an adopted extended family of sorts, all of whom are available for advice, help, consolation, and celebration.

The Rescue JRT

There is one more alternative: the rescue JRT. You may find it doubly rewarding to provide a loving home for an adult JRT who has fallen upon hard times. Unfortunately, the JRTCA Russell Rescue commonly has more JRTs than homes. Most of these dogs simply had the misfortune of being owned by somebody who either could not cope with the typical JRT personality, or who bought a dog on a whim. The only thing worse for these dogs than not getting adopted is to be adopted by another unprepared or uncommitted family. Don't take your decision to get a rescue JRT any more lightly than your original decision to get a JRT. For the address of Russell Rescue, see page 98.

Much as you may be tempted to rush in and save one of these souls, take the time to first ascertain why that particular JRT did not work out for its former owner. If you are a new dog owner, it may be best to leave a dog with behavior problems for a more experienced owner to deal with. Speak with a veterinarian, knowledgeable dog trainer, or behaviorist and ask what the treatment and prognosis is for any behavior disorder. Most often, you will find that their only crime was being a typical JRT.

Other Sources

Most dogs are not obtained through breed clubs, rescue organizations, or dog shows. Instead, they are usually obtained through friends, neighbors, newspaper ads, and pet shops.

The chances of your friend or neighbor being a knowledgeable JRT breeder are remote. Although there are exceptions, too many newspaper ads are placed by backyard breeders who typically know no more about breeding JRTs than to put a male and female together and see what comes out. A pet shop should be able to provide the same information about a puppy that you would get directly from the breeder: the pedigrees and health records of the parents; whether the puppy was raised around loving people; how long it stayed with the mother; and so forth.

Breeder Danger Signals

• Breeders who use incorrect terms, such as thoroughbreds, full-blooded,

Jack Russell terriers come in many types. The popular short-legged Jack Russell is not one of the correct types, however, although they still make charming pets.

spaded, or papered, or boast of a "long pedigree."
• Breeders of more than two different breeds of dogs. Most dedicated breeders spend years studying one breed and could never have the resources to do justice to several breeds. Multi-breed breeders are usually small scale puppy mills.
• Breeders of more than two or three litters per year, unless they are one of the top kennels in the country.
• Breeders who can't compare their dogs to the JRT standard, or don't know the standard.
• Breeders unfamiliar with any JRT health concerns.
• Breeders who insist you view the puppies at a place other than their home.
• Breeders who have no photos or videotapes of both parents and other relatives.
• Breeders who have no pedigree on hand.
• Breeders without registered stock.
• Breeders who do not allow you to visit the dam of a litter.
• Breeders who insist on "puppy-back" agreements, requiring you to breed your dog and give them puppies from the resulting litter.
• Breeders who ask you no questions.
• Breeders who think JRTs are ideal for everyone.

Children, horses, and Jack Russells make a natural team, as long as the child is taught to respect the dog's feelings and to treat it with responsibility and fairness.

dogs, why you want a Jack Russell terrier, what you know about living with one, and what living arrangements you have planned for the dog. Consider the following questions:

1. Ask about the parents. Are they JRTCA or JRTBA registered? If they are not JRTCA registered because they were of insufficient quality, then they should never have been allowed to produce puppies. If they are not registered because the breeder just didn't care to, this is another bad sign because it shows a careless attitude on the part of the breeder.

2. What kind of temperaments do the parents and the puppies have? Have the parents or puppies had any health problems? Have the parents been tested for any hereditary problems? If the breeder states that the parents have been tested for eye problems or deafness, then this is an excellent sign, but most JRT breeders don't screen because problems are so rare. Ask questions such as, "Why did you breed the litter?" "How did you choose the sire?"

3. Ask about the terms of sale. Don't fall in love with a puppy and then have to walk away because an agreement could not be reached. There are several possibilities, the easiest being that you will pay a set amount (usually cash) and receive full ownership. Registration papers and pedigree should never cost extra. Sometimes breeders will insist upon having a pet puppy neutered before supplying the papers. If you are making installment payments, the breeder will probably retain the papers or a co-ownership until the last installment. Sometimes a breeder will insist upon co-owning the puppy permanently. If any co-ownership involves future breeding of the puppy (especially a female) and "puppy-back" agreements, you probably should shy away. If the co-ownership is for insurance that the

- Breeders who tell you that you can make your money back by breeding your JRT.
- Breeders who will not take the dog back at any time in its life should you not be able to keep it. Good breeders care about the welfare of the dog for its entire life, not just until it walks out the door.
- Cheap puppies. Expect to pay from $350 to $600 for a good quality JRT. Males and females should cost the same.

Questions, Questions

Focus your attention on breeders who can boast of registered and titled stock, home-raised pups, and a willingness to discuss both pros and cons of the breed. A good breeder should ask you about your previous history with dog will be returned to the breeder in the event you cannot keep it, such an agreement is usually acceptable. Any such terms should be in writing.

Any time you buy a puppy, it should be done so with the stipulation that purchase is pending a health check (at your expense) by your veterinarian. The breeder should furnish you with a complete medical history including dates of vaccinations and worming.

Selecting a Puppy

Once you have narrowed down your list, if possible arrange to visit the breeder. Most modern "kennels" are a collection of only a few dogs that are first of all the breeder's pets. However large or small the operation, look for facilities that are clean and safe. Again, these are clues about the care given your prospective puppy. Although it is virtually impossible to keep a litter of JRT puppies from creating an ongoing catastrophe, any messes should be obviously new. Old droppings are a sign of poor hygiene, and poor hygiene is a precursor to poor health.

The adults should be clean, groomed, and in apparent good health. They should neither try to attack you nor cower from you. Look to the adults for the dog your puppy will become. If you don't care for their looks or temperaments, say good-bye. Do make allowances for the dam's ordeal of carrying and nursing, however. Ask to see a picture of her before breeding. If the sire is not on the premises, ask to see pictures of him as well. If such pictures are not available, the warning lights should go on. A reputable breeder will have so many pictures not only of the parents, but other dogs far removed in the pedigree, that you will wish you never asked!

Always go to view the puppies prepared to leave without one if you don't see exactly what you want. Remember, no good breeder wants you to take a

"Pick me, pick me, pick me!"

puppy you are not 110 percent crazy about. This is not something you can trade in once you find what you really want. Don't lead the breeder on if you

Cradle the pup under its chest and rear, and hold it securely next to your own body.

Pay careful attention to the breeder's instructions. During your initial visit, both you and the breeder will be evaluating one another.

visit. In addition, your entire family should know how to properly hold a puppy. Never pick a puppy up by its legs or head or tail; cradle the puppy with both hands, one under the chest, the other under the hindquarters, and with the side of the pup secure against your chest. Keep a firm hold lest the pup try to squirm out of your arms unexpectedly. When placing the pup down, make sure all four legs are on the ground before letting go. Even at a young age mistreatment or negligence might have damaged your puppy's temperament or health, so watch the breeder to see that he or she treats the pups with love and gentleness.

Picking the Healthiest JRT Pup

As you finally look upon this family of busy little bodies, you may suddenly find it very difficult to be objective. How will you ever decide which one is best for you? If you want a show or field puppy, let the breeder decide. In fact, the breeder knows the puppies' personalities better than you will in the short time you can evaluate them, so listen carefully to any suggestions the breeder has even for a pet. It is human nature to pick "extremes," but most breeders would advise against choosing either the boldest or quietest JRT puppy, or any pup that acts shy.

Several puppy aptitude tests have been popularized throughout the years. Most follow-up data has unfortunately indicated that they have little predictive value, so if you are determined to test the pups but your heart is still with a pup that didn't score on top, go with your heart. However, before doing any deciding between pups, first decide if this is the litter for you.
• By eight weeks of age, JRT pups should look like little Jack Russell terriers.
• Dark nose pigmentation, absent at birth, should be present by this age.

have decided against a purchase; there may be another buyer in line.

Don't be secretive if you are considering more than one breeder. Breeders talk to each other and will find out you are comparison shopping anyway, and there is nothing wrong with comparing. Just don't visit from one breeder to another on the same day, and certainly do not visit the animal shelter beforehand. Puppies are vulnerable to many deadly diseases that you can transmit by way of your hands, clothes, and shoes. How tragic it would be if the breeder's invitation for you to view their darlings ended up killing them.

Handling the Puppies

These puppies are fragile little beings, and you must be extremely careful where you step and how you handle them. If you have children with you, don't allow them to run around or play with the puppies unsupervised. In fact, a good breeder will send you away puppyless if your children can't control themselves suitably during even a short

- Feet and knuckles will be disproportionately large, but otherwise the pup should appear balanced, with front and rear legs approximately the same length.
- When viewed from the front or rear, the legs should be nearly parallel to each other, neither cow-hocked in the rear nor "east-west" in the front.
- Normal Jack Russell terrier puppies are active, friendly, curious, and attentive. If they are apathetic or sleeping, it could be because they have just eaten, but it could also be because they are sickly.
- The puppies should be clean, with no missing hair, crusted or reddened skin, or signs of parasites. Eyes, ears, and nose should be free of discharge. Pups should not be coughing, sneezing, or vomiting.
- Examine the eyelids to ensure that the lids or lashes don't roll in on the eye.
- The teeth should be straight and meet up evenly, with the top incisors just overlapping the bottom incisors.
- The gums should be pink; pale gums may indicate anemia.
- The area around the anus should have no hint of irritation or recent diarrhea.
- Pick up a fold of skin. It should "pop" back into place, adhering to the body. If it stays "tented" up, the pup could be dehydrated, which can result from repeated diarrhea or vomiting.
- Puppies should not be thin or potbellied. The belly should have no large bumps indicating an umbilical hernia.
- By the age of 12 weeks, male puppies should have both testicles descended in the scrotum.

If the puppy of your choice is limping, or exhibits any of the above symptoms, express your concern and ask to either come back the following week to see if it has improved, or to have your veterinarian examine it.

You may still find it nearly impossible to decide which little perpetual motion machine will be yours. Don't worry—no matter which one you choose, as long as it is from a good breeder and background, and you do your part to help it reach its potential, you will hit the jackpot of Jack Russells.

Your Jack Russell Terrier at Home

After finally finding your JRT pup, it's only natural to want to bring it home right away. But take a minute to look around your house. Is it really ready to withstand a juvenile Jack attack? It will be a lot easier to get it into terrier-proof shape now than it will be when you have a little puppy underfoot undoing everything just as fast as you can do it! So channel your excitement and make sure everything is just perfect and waiting for the new addition.

If you are contemplating bringing your pup home as a Christmas present, think again! The heartwarming scene you may have imagined of the

As appealing a picture as it may be in your dreams, a puppy for Christmas is more likely to be a catastrophe—unless it is the only present planned and not a surprise.

children discovering the puppy asleep among the other gifts beneath the tree on Christmas morning is not realistic. The real scene is more often that of a crying, confused puppy who may have vented its anxiety on the other gifts and left you some additional "gifts" of its own beneath the tree! Don't bring a new puppy into the hectic chaos of Christmas morning. Not only does this add to what is bound to be a very confusing and intimidating transition for your JRT, but a puppy should not be expected to compete with all of the toys and games that children may be receiving. Every pup needs the undivided attention of its new family at this crucial time in its life. Instead, a photograph or videotape of your special Jack Russell-to-be, or a stocking of puppy paraphernalia, should provide sufficient surprise, and give the whole family time to prepare.

Keeping One Step Ahead

The number one JRT safety item is a securely fenced yard. Jack Russell terriers are notorious ramblers. In today's world of automobiles and suburbs, a loose dog is at best an unwelcome visitor and, more often, a dead dog. JRTs are gifted jumpers, climbers, burrowers, and squeezers. They will find the smallest vulnerable spot in any fence.

The JRT's gift for digging can enable it to tunnel to freedom with uncanny speed. Not only should the bottom of your fence extend well underground, but you should also lay wire on, or just under, the ground extending for a few feet inside the yard. This prevents the dog from digging directly down next to the fence.

Many dogs are actually inadvertently taught to escape by their owners. Perhaps the new owner has an old fence, and decides to wait and see if it will hold the dog. When the dog squeezes out of the weakest spots, the owner patches those. But now the dog has learned that the fence is not impenetrable, and seeks out another, less obvious weak spot. Finally the dog is creating its own weak spots, jumping Olympic heights, burrowing to China, and squeezing through holes that you would swear couldn't possibly accommodate a dog with bones—and its owner taught it to do it. If you wanted your JRT to learn to squeeze through small passages or jump great heights, wouldn't you do so a little at a time? Then why use the same tactic to teach your dog *not* to squeeze through? If you want your dog to stay in the yard, make the yard Jack Russell terrier-proof from the very beginning.

Your fence must not only be strong enough to keep your dog in, but to keep stray dogs out. This is why the "invisible fences" that keep your dog in the yard are less than optimal. They only work with a dog wearing a special shock collar that is activated by the buried boundary wire. They can't keep out stray dogs that aren't wearing such a collar. In addition, an excited or particularly strong-willed dog—such as a Jack Russell!—can just "grit its teeth" and charge right through the boundary.

Dangers in the Yard

There can still be dangers within the yard. If you leave your JRT alone in your yard, lock your gate, and take precautions to not make your defenseless friend a target for Russell rustlers. Check for poisonous plants, bushes with sharp, broken branches at JRT eye

Temptation! Even if your dog doesn't like to swim, it should be taught how to get out of any pool it may be near.

Toys, toys, and more toys—a few of their favorite things.

29

level, and trees with dead branches or heavy fruits in danger of falling. If you have a pool, be aware that, although dogs are natural swimmers, a little JRT cannot pull itself up a swimming pool wall, and it can drown. Plug up any holes leading under the house that might lead a terrier into temptation.

Dangers Inside

Terrier-proofing your home has two goals: protecting your dog, and protecting your home. The first step is to do everything you would do to baby-proof your home. Get down at puppy level and see what dangers beckon.
• Puppies love to chew electrical cords in half, and even lick outlets. This can result in death from shock, severe burns, and loss of jaw and tongue tissue.
• Jumping up on an unstable object (such as a bookcase) could cause it to come crashing down, perhaps crushing the puppy.
• Do not allow the puppy near the edges of high decks, balconies, or staircases. Use temporary plastic fencing or chicken wire in dangerous areas.
• Doors can be a hidden danger area. Everyone in your family must be made to understand the danger of slamming a door, which could catch a small dog and break a leg—or worse. Use doorstops to ensure that the wind does not suddenly blow doors shut, or that the puppy does not go behind the door to play. This can be a danger, because the gap on the hinged side of the door can catch and break a little leg if the door is closed. Be especially cautious with swinging doors; a puppy may try to push one open, become caught, try to back out, and strangle. Clear glass doors may not be seen, and the puppy could be injured running into them. *Never* close a garage door with a JRT running about. Finally, doors leading to unfenced outdoor areas

Poisonous Plants
azaleas
castor bean
corn cockle
English holly berries
foxglove
Jerusalem cherry
jessamine
jimson weed
milkweed
mistletoe
oleander
philodendron
rattlebox
rhododendron
water hemlock

should be kept securely shut. A screen door is a vital safety feature; Jack Russells are adept at streaking between your legs to freedom when you open the front door.

Household JRT Killers

The following are potentially lethal to your inquisitive pet:
• rodent, snail, and insect baits
• antifreeze
• household cleaners
• toilet fresheners
• drugs
• chocolate (especially baker's chocolate)
• nuts, bolts, pennies
• pins and needles, and, in fact, anything in a sewing basket
• chicken bones or any bone that could be swallowed

Household Furnishings and Personal Belongings

A JRT pup left alone can be an accomplished one-dog demolition team. Leather furniture is the world's biggest rawhide chewy to a puppy, and wicker can provide hours of chewing enjoyment (and danger to the dog from splintering). Anything with fur is definite terrier bait. Puppies particularly like to chew items that carry your scent. Shoes, eyeglasses, and clothing must be kept out of the youngster's reach. Remove anything breakable that you value from your JRT's reach. Remove books and papers. No need for a costly paper shredder when you have a puppy! Move any houseplants that you would like to survive. The ingenuity of the Jack Russell terrier is never so obvious as when it is looking for trouble.

Your carpets (at least in the area between the cage and the door) can be covered with small washable rugs or indoor/outdoor carpeting until your puppy is housebroken. If you use an X-pen (see page 32), cover the floor beneath it with thick plastic (an old shower curtain works well), and then add towels or washable rugs for traction and absorbancy.

Jack Tack

When it comes to accessories for your JRT, it's not really true that "all you add is love" (but you'll need lots of that, too)! The best sources for equipment are large pet stores, dog shows, and discount pet catalogs. Your welcome basket should include:
• **buckle collar**—to wear around the house
• **choke collar or harness**—safer for walking on lead
• **leash**—nylon, web, or leather—never chain! An adjustable show lead is good for puppies.
• **lightweight retractable leash**—better for older adult; be sure not to drop the leash as it may retract toward the pup and frighten it.
• **stainless steel flat-bottomed food and water bowls**—avoid plastic; it can cause allergic reactions and hold germs.
• **cage**—just large enough for an adult dog to stand up in without having to lower its head.
• **exercise pen**—tall enough that an adult dog can't jump over, or preferably with a top.

• **toys**—latex squeakies, fleece type toys, ball, stuffed animals, stuffed socks. Make sure the toys have no parts, such as squeakers or plastic eyes, that can be pulled off and swallowed.
• **chewbones**—the equivalent of a teething ring for babies
• **anti-chew preparations,** such as Bitter Apple. The unpleasant taste discourages pups from chewing on items sprayed with it.
• **baby gate(s)**—better than a shut door for placing parts of your home off-limits.
• **brush and comb**
• **nail clippers**
• **poop scoop**—two-piece rake-type is best for grass.
• **dog shampoo** (see page 62 for choices)
• **first aid kit** (see page 71 for contents)
• **sweater**—for cold climates.
• **food**—start with the same food the pup is currently eating.
• **dog bed**—a round fleece-lined cat bed is perfect, but you can also use the bottom of a plastic cage, or any cozy box with padding. Wicker will most likely be chewed to shreds.
• **camera and film!** (Telephoto lens is a big help.)

The Den

A cage (or crate) is the canine equivalent of an infant's crib. It is a place for naptime, a place where you can leave your pup without worry that it will hurt itself or your home. It is not a place for punishment, nor is it a storage box for your dog when you're through playing with it. Place the cage in a corner of a quiet room, but not too far from the rest of the family. Place the pup in the cage when it begins to fall asleep, and it will become accustomed to using it as its bed. Be sure to place a soft blanket in the bottom. Also, by taking the pup directly from the cage to the outdoors upon awakening, the cage will be one

Give your Jack Russell something safe to chew, and both of you will be a lot happier.

of the handiest housebreaking aids at your disposal.

Many new dog owners are initially appalled at the idea of putting their pet in a cage as though it were some wild beast. At times, though, any puppy can seem like a wild beast, and a cage is one way to save your home from ruination and yourself from insanity. A cage can also provide a quiet haven for your youngster. Just as you hopefully find peace and security as you sink into your own bed at night, your pup needs a place that it can call its own, a place it can seek out whenever the need for rest and solitude arises. Used properly, your JRT will come to think of its cage not as way to keep itself in, but as a way to keep others out!

The X-Pen

An exercise pen (or "X-pen") fulfills many of the same functions as a cage. X-pens are transportable wire folding "playpens" for dogs, typically about 4′ × 4′ (1.2 m). X-pens are the perfect solution when you must be gone for a long time, because the pup can relieve itself on paper in one corner, sleep on a soft bed in the other, and frolic with its toys all over! It's like having a little yard inside. Sometimes even the most devoted owners need a break from the constant antics of their JRT. The X-pen provides a safe time-out area when you just need some quiet time for yourself. But before leaving your pup in an X-pen, make sure that it cannot jump or climb out. Covers are available for incorrigible escapees.

The Run of the House

Don't let your JRT puppy have the run of the entire house. Choose an easily puppy-proofed room where you spend a lot of time, preferably one that is close to a door leading outside. Kitchens and dens are usually ideal. When you must leave your dog for some time, you may wish to place it in a cage, X-pen, secure room, or outdoor kennel. Bathrooms have the disadvantage of being so confining and isolated that puppies may become destructive; garages have the disadvantage of also housing many poisonous items.

Don't get a JRT and banish it to the far corners of the yard. Although your dog can spend a good part of its time

"You want ME to bring you your slippers?"

A rough-coated pup.

outdoors in nice weather, why get a dog at all if you don't plan on welcoming it as a real member of your family? Your JRT will want to be in the thick of things, and participate in everything your family does. So plan for your dog to be quartered in the house where it can be around activity, but not necessarily always underfoot. If you plan on leaving your dog in the yard for extended periods, you must provide a snug doghouse.

The Scoop

The least glamorous, yet essential, item on your list is the poop scoop. What goes in must come out, and hopefully in your yard. Many dog owners never step foot in their own backyards because of dog excrement. Dogs raised in unclean yards grow used to stepping in feces and will continue to do so with reckless abandon their entire lives, an especially disgusting trait if your dog sleeps in your bed or tends to jump up on you. Start early

and keep your yard meticulously scooped, except for a sample pile in the area you wish the dog to continue using as its toilet area. Don't make your JRT live in a mine field.

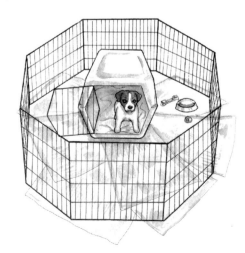

The X-pen is a safe yard within the home.

HOW-TO:
Coping with Terrier Terrors

Terriers are known mischief makers, and Jack Russell terriers are no exception. Indeed, this is one of the most endearing traits of the breed. But often misbehavior causes problems for their family or themselves, sometimes creating an intolerable situation. Despairing owners blame the dog, and these dogs often end up at the animal shelter. Yet most of these problems can be avoided or cured.

Misuse of punishment is a major cause of continuing problems. If punishment doesn't work the first time, why do owners think that it will work the second, third, or fourth time?

Jumping Up

Puppies naturally greet their mother and other adult dogs by licking them around the corners of their mouth. This behavior translates to humans, but in order to reach your face they need to jump up on you. Sometimes owners love this

Teach your Jack Russell to stay on the ground for greetings by kneeling down to its level.

display of affection, but not when they are all dressed up or when company comes over. Of course, you can't expect your JRT to know the difference. Instead, teach your dog to sit and stay, and then be sure to kneel down to its level for greetings. When your JRT does jump up, simply say *"No"* and step backward, so that its paws meet only air. Teaching your dog a special command that lets it know it's OK to jump up (when you're in your bum clothes) can actually help it determine the difference.

Shutting your dog in another room when guests arrive will only make it more crazed to greet people, and ultimately worsen the problem. The more people it gets a chance to greet politely, the less excited it will be about meeting new people, and the less inclined it will be to jump up. Have your guests kneel and greet your sitting JRT.

Barking

Having a doggy doorbell can be handy, but there is a difference between a dog that will warn you of a suspicious stranger and one that will warn you of the presence of oxygen in the air. The surest way to make your neighbors dislike your dog is to let it create a racket. Allow your JRT to bark momentarily at strangers, and then call it to you and praise it for quiet behavior, distracting it with an obedience exercise if need be.

Isolated dogs will often bark as a means of getting attention and alleviating loneliness. Even if the attention gained includes

punishment, the dog will continue to bark in order to obtain the temporary presence of the owner. The simplest solution is to move the dog's quarters to a less isolated location. For example, if barking occurs when your pup is put to bed, move its bed into your bedroom. If this is not possible, the pup's quiet behavior must be rewarded by the owner's presence, working up to gradually longer and longer periods. The distraction of a special chew toy, given only at bedtime, may help alleviate barking. The pup that must spend the day home alone is a greater challenge. Again, the simplest solution is to change the situation, perhaps by adding another animal—a good excuse to get two JRTs! But warning: Some Jack Russells also like to bark when playing!

Ultrasonic collars emit an irritating sound every time your dog barks, and can often persuade a dog to stop barking. Anti-bark shock collars give the dog a mild electrical shock with each bark, and can be even more effective. In both cases you must be careful that the collars not respond to other dogs barking!

Digging

JRTs are naturally interested in what may lay beneath the earth (after all, the word "terrier" is derived from "terra," denoting these dogs' inclination to go to ground). Don't get a JRT if you can't stand the sight of holes. The only cure for digging is a lot of exercise and a lot of supervision, and fencing off those parts of the yard that you absolutely can't tolerate

Separation anxiety is characterized by lapses in house-breaking, nervous behavior, and destruction around doors and windows, particularly chewed and scratched walls, door jambs, and rugs.

The proper therapy is treatment of the dog's fear of being left alone. This is done by leaving the dog alone for very short periods of time and gradually working to longer periods, taking care to never allow the dog to become anxious during any session. When you must leave the dog for long periods during the conditioning program, leave it in a different part of the house than the one in which the conditioning sessions take place, so that you don't undo all of your work by letting the dog become over-stressed by your long absence.

In either case, when you return home, no matter what the condition of the house or apartment, greet the dog calmly or even ignore it for a few minutes, to emphasize the point that being left was really no big deal. Then have the dog perform a simple trick or obedience exercise so that you have an excuse to praise it. It takes a lot of patience, and often a whole lot of self-control, but it's not fair to you or your dog to let this situation continue.

being turned into a moonscape. Remedies based on harsh corrections are not successful.

Car Chasing

Keep the dog in the yard! JRTs have a weakness for rolling wheels. If you must try to effect a cure, either stop the car as soon as chasing begins, or carry along a hi-tech long-distance squirt gun and spray the dog from the car.

Home Destruction

Many a Jack Russell owner has returned home to a disaster area and suspected that Jack the Ripper must have broken in the house. JRTs may be small, but they can be talented home redecorators.

Note: Dogs never destroy out of spite.

Puppies are natural demolition dogs, and the best cure is adulthood, although adult dogs still may dig or destroy items through frustration or boredom. The best way to deal with these dogs is to provide both physical interaction (such as chasing a ball) and mental interaction (such as practicing a few simple obedience commands) on a daily basis.

More commonly, destructive behavior in an adult dog is due to separation anxiety. Dogs are highly social animals, and being left alone is an extremely stressful condition for many of them. They react by becoming agitated and trying to escape from confinement and, in fact, most of their destructive behavior is focused around doors and windows. Most owners believe the dog is "spiting" them for leaving it, and they then punish the dog. Unfortunately, punishment is ineffective because it actually increases the anxiety level of the dog, as it comes to both look forward to and dread its owner's return.

Welcome home! No matter how upset you may be, ignore the dog when you come home. Punishment won't help separation anxiety.

The Welcome Wagon

Schedule your new pup's homecoming during a period when you will have several days to spend at home but don't make the mistake of spending every moment with the new dog. Accustom the pup to short times away from you, so that when you do leave the house it won't be too upset.

If possible, bring a family member to hold and comfort the puppy on the ride home. If it is a long ride, bring a cage. Be sure to take plenty of towels in case it gets carsick. Never let a new puppy roam around the car, where it can cause, and have, accidents. The ride home with you may be the puppy's first time in a car, and its first time away from the security of its home and former family. Spend some time at the breeder's house while the puppy gets acquainted with you, and listen carefully to the breeder's instructions.

Your pup will learn a new name quickly if it means food or fun is on the way. Be careful about the name you choose; for example, "Nomad" sounds like both "no" and "bad," and could confuse a dog. Test your chosen name to be sure that it does not sound like a reprimand or command.

When you get home, put the puppy on lead and carry it to the spot you have decided will be its toilet area. Once the puppy relieves itself, praise and give it a tidbit, let it explore a little, and then offer it a small meal. Once the puppy has eaten, it will probably have to relieve itself again, so take it back out to the toilet area and remember to praise and give a tidbit for a job well done. When your pup begins to act sleepy, place it in its cage so that it knows this is its special bed. A stuffed toy, ticking clock, or plastic milk bottle filled with warm water may help alleviate some of the anxiety of being left alone. You may wish to place the cage in your bedroom for this first

Inside or outside, Jack Russells seek out vantage points from which to survey their kingdoms.

Don't be surprised if your nimble Jack Russell climbs trees. Cats and Jack Russells can coexist peacefully, but must be introduced carefully.

night so that the puppy may be comforted by your presence. Remember, this is the scariest thing that has ever happened in your puppy's short life; it has been uprooted from the security of a mother, littermates, and loving breeder, so you must be comforting and reassuring on this crucial first night.

Important: The first day with you is not the time for all the neighbors to come visiting. You want your pup to know who its new family members will be, and more people will only add to the youngster's confusion. Nor is it the time for rough-and-tumble play, which could scare the puppy. Introductions to other family pets might also be better postponed. Why make a confusing and stressful experience even more overwhelming?

Creating a Civilized Housedog

Your pup now faces the transition from canine litter member to human family member. Every day will be full of novel experiences and new rules. Your pup is naturally inquisitive and will need for you to guide it toward becoming a well-mannered member of the household.

Off-Limits Training

You should have decided before your puppy came home what parts of your home will be off limits. Make sure that every family member understands the rules, and that they understand that sneaking the puppy onto off-limit furniture, for example, is not doing the puppy any favor at all. Your puppy will naturally want to explore every nook and cranny of your house. Part of the pup's exploratory tools are its teeth, and any chewed items left in its wake are your fault, not your pup's—you are the one who should have known better. Harsh corrections are no more effective than a tap on the nose along with a firm *"No,"* and removal of the item.

JRTs love to be up on furniture and other high places, but if you don't want to allow such behavior start early. A harsh *"No!"* and firm but gentle push away from the furniture should let it realize that this is neither acceptable nor rewarding behavior. Don't fling the pup off the furniture, or use mousetraps on furniture surfaces; both practices are dangerous and a terrible idea unless you like emergency visits to the vet. There are several more humane items (available through pet catalogs) that emit a loud tone when a dog jumps on furniture, but these should not be necessary if you train your young puppy gently and consistently from the beginning.

Housebreaking

Unsupervised freedom: The number one housebreaking mistake made by most puppy owners is to give their puppies too much unsupervised freedom in the house. All canines have a natural desire to avoid soiling their denning area. As soon as young wolves are able to walk, they will teeter out of their den to relieve themselves away from their bedding. Since you are using a cage for your puppy's den, your JRT will naturally try to avoid soiling it. Puppies have very weak control over their bowels, however, so if you don't take them to their elimination area often, they may not be able to avoid soiling. Furthermore, if the cage is too large, the puppy may simply step away from the area it sleeps in and relieve itself at the other end of the cage. An overly large cage can be divided with a secure barrier until the puppy is larger or housebroken. Even so, just like the wolf cubs, your puppy may step just outside the door of the cage and eliminate there because to the pup, that fulfills the natural requirement of not soiling the den. The puppy has failed to realize that it has just soiled *your* den. And the more the pup soils in a partic-

ular spot, the more it is likely to return to that same spot.

Accidents: To avoid accidents, learn to predict when your puppy will have to relieve itself. Immediately after awakening, and soon after heavy drinking or playing, your puppy will urinate. You will probably have to carry a younger baby outside to get it to the toilet area on time. Right after eating, or if nervous, your puppy will have to defecate. Circling, whining, sniffing, and generally acting worried usually signals that defecation is imminent. Even if the puppy starts to relieve itself, quickly but calmly scoop the pup up and carry it outside (the surprise of being picked up will usually cause the puppy to stop in midstream, so to speak). You can add a firm *"No,"* but yelling and swatting are neither necessary nor effective. When the puppy does relieve itself in its outside toilet, remember to heap on the praise and let your JRT pup know how pleased you are. Adding a food treat really gets the point across. Keep some in a jar near the door and always accompany your pup outside so that you can reward it.

Puppies tend to relieve themselves in areas they can smell that they have used before. This is why it is so critical to never let the pup have an accident indoors; if it does, clean and deodorize the spot thoroughly (using a nonammonia-based cleanser) and block the pup's access to that area.

Punishment: The number two housebreaking mistake made by dog owners is overuse of punishment. Even if you catch your dog in the act, overly enthusiastic correction tends only to teach the dog not to relieve itself in your presence, even when outside. This is why you should reward the pup with a tidbit when it *does* relieve itself outside. Punishment does not make clear what is desired behavior, but reward makes it clear very quickly. Punishing a dog for a mess it has made earlier is totally fruitless; it only succeeds in convincing the dog that every once in a while, for no apparent reason, you are apt to go insane and attack it. It is a perfect recipe for ruining a trusting relationship. That "guilty" look you may think your dog is exhibiting is really fear that you have once again lost your mind.

Leaving your pup outdoors: If you cannot be with your puppy for an extended period, you may wish to leave it outside (weather permitting) so that it will not be forced to have an indoor accident. If this is not possible, you may have to paper train your puppy. Place newspapers on the far side of the room (or X-pen), away from the puppy's bed or water bowl; near a door to the outside is best. Place the puppy on the papers as soon as it starts to relieve itself. Paper training is a last resort and it is best to forego it entirely, if possible. It would be better if you could arrange to have someone let your dog out every four hours or so.

As soon as you are convinced your precocious puppy is housebroken, it will sometimes, unfortunately, take a giant step backward and convince you there is no link between its brain and bowels. No matter how wonderful and smart your JRT is, it probably will not have full control over its elimination until it is around six months of age, but keep up your training and things really will get better.

Housesoiling

There are many reasons why a dog might soil the house:
• Commonly, the dog was never completely housebroken to start with, and so you must begin housebreaking all over again.
* Sometimes a housebroken dog will be forced to soil the house because of a bout of diarrhea, and afterwards will continue to soil in the same area. If this happens, restrict that area from the dog, and revert to basic housebreaking lessons once again. Remember to thoroughly clean the areas with a deodorizer (available at pet stores) to eliminate the odor.
• Submissive dogs may urinate upon greeting you; punishment only makes this "submissive urination" worse. For these dogs, keep greetings calm, don't bend over or otherwise dominate the dog, and usually this can be outgrown.
• Some dogs defecate or urinate due to the stress of separation anxiety; you must treat the anxiety to cure the symptom.
• Older dogs may simply not have the bladder control that they had as youngsters; paper training or a doggy door is the best solution for them.
• Older spayed females may "dribble"; ask your veterinarian about estrogen supplementation that may help.
• Dogs may have lost control due to a bladder infection; several small urine spots (especially if bloody or dark) are a sign that a trip to the veterinarian is needed.
• Male dogs may "lift their leg" inside the house as a means of marking it as theirs. Castration will usually solve this problem; otherwise, diligent deodorizing and the use of some dog-deterring odorants (available at pet stores) may help.

Behavior Problems

Hyperactivity

Most dogs labeled hyperactive by their owners are really not, but just underexercised normal dogs for their breed. The JRT is an active breed and you need to find ways to channel its energy. Set times for walks, games, and obedience. Although your dog will slow down with age, this is years in the future. This is why it is so important to get to know the JRT before inviting one into your home. In severe cases you may wish to consult with your dog's breeder, other JRT owners,

"Howdy!" The spotted dog displays dominant behavior to the white, submissive dog.

Russell Rescue (see page 98), or your veterinarian. If they agree your dog is simply a normal JRT (and it probably is), you can either wait for age to slow it down, or find it a home with someone already familiar and happy with Jack Russell high spirits.

Fearfulness

Despite their generally fearless attitude, JRTs can develop phobias and other fears. Never push your dog into situations that might overwhelm it. Never force a dog that is afraid of strangers to be petted by someone it doesn't know; it in no way helps the dog overcome its fear and is a good way for the stranger to get bitten. Strangers should be asked to ignore shy dogs, even when approached by the dog. Dogs seem to fear the attention of a stranger more than they fear the strangers themselves.

When the dog gets braver, have the stranger offer it a tidbit, at first while not even looking at the dog. A program of gradual desensitization, with the dog exposed to the frightening person or thing and then rewarded for calm behavior, is time consuming but the best way to alleviate any fear.

Never coddle your dog when it acts afraid, because it reinforces the behavior. It is always useful if your JRT knows a few simple commands (see HOW-TO: Basic Commands, page 54); performing these exercises correctly gives you a reason to praise the dog and also increases the dog's sense of security because it knows what is expected of it. Whether it is a fear of strangers, dogs, car rides, thunder, or being left alone, the concept is the same—never hurry, and never push the dog to the point that it is afraid.

Aggression

Jack Russell terrier teeth can wreak considerable damage on human skin. The best cure for aggression is prevention, and the best prevention is to obtain your pup from a reputable breeder and to raise it with kindness, gentleness, and firmness, never encouraging biting nor displays of dominance, and never punishing for deeds the dog cannot comprehend. Expose the pup to kind strangers from a young age, and make these interactions pleasurable.

Guests and Children

Dogs that are tied up just out of reach of activity are prime candidates for biters. Dogs that are hustled out of the room when guests arrive, or out of the family activities when a new baby arrives, will sometimes bite out of resentment. Teach your JRT to look forward to guests and children by . rewarding proper behavior, such as sitting and staying, in their presence, and by having them offer the dog a treat. A drastic measure is to withhold attention from the dog except in the presence of guests or the baby, so that the dog associates being with them as something that brings itself attention and rewards.

Of course, it should hardly be mentioned that no baby or child should be allowed to play roughly with or tease your JRT; one could hardly blame a small dog that growls or bites out of self-defense, but one could blame its owner for letting the situation develop.

Direct Eye Contact

Unlike in humans, where direct eye contact is seen as a sign of sincerity, staring a dog directly in the eye is interpreted by the dog as a threat. It can cause a fearful dog to bite out of what it perceives as self-defense, and is responsible for many dog bites.

Other Dogs

Cocky JRTs are sometimes known to challenge strange dogs when good sense should tell them they are overmatched. Keeping your terrier on lead and out of reach of other dogs is the best prevention. More problematic is the case where two dogs that live together do not get along. Dogs may be vying for dominance, and fights will occur until one dog emerges as the clear victor. But even in cases where one dog is dominant, fights may erupt when both are competing for the owner's attention. The dominant dog expects to get that attention before the subordinate, but being fair-minded owners, we tend to give attention equally, or to even favor the "under-dog." This can be interpreted by the dominant dog as an uprising by the subordinate dog, who is then attacked. This is one case where playing favorites (to the dominant dog) will actually be a favor to the subordinate dog in the long run!

Stopping a dogfight: If a fight is about to break out try to distract the dogs (perhaps with the promise of a walk) or spray them with water. Yelling or grabbing tends to escalate the tension and increase the chances of a fight. If a fight ensues, douse the combatants with water, or throw blankets over each of them. Fighting dogs have bad aim, so keep away from those teeth! If two people are present, as a last resort, grab each dog by its hind legs and pull it off the ground, holding it away from your body. This is a last resort because it could injure the dog's hindquarters. Some people keep a tub of water handy and actually throw the fighters in it in order to separate them. Of course, if the dogs aren't next to the tub at the time, it is of little help. Others keep a cattle prod on hand with which to break up fighters. The cattle prod gives the dog a shock, which usually distracts it, but it can also goad it on to more vigorous fighting.

Introducing new dogs: When introducing new dogs, it is best if both are taken to a neutral site so that territoriality does not provoke aggression. Two people walking the dogs beside each other as they would on a regular walk is an ideal way for dogs to accept each other. However, some JRTs are more aggressive when on lead, so make sure there is something to interest both dogs besides each other. If you are still worried, muzzle both dogs before letting them loose together.

Other Animals

JRTs can be trustworthy around farm stock and household pets, including cats, but don't tempt them with hamsters and rats. Introduce your JRT to your cat gradually, inside the house. The dog should be held on leash initially, and the cat prevented from running, which would elicit a chase response in the dog. If the dog is fed every time the cat appears, it will come to appreciate the cat's presence. Don't leave them unsupervised unless you are absolutely sure of your JRT's good intentions.

Hit the Road

A car trip with your JRT can be a rewarding experience, as the two of you join together for an adventurous odyssey. A dog gives you a good excuse to stop and enjoy the scenery up close, and maybe even get some exercise along the way.

A trip with your JRT can also be a nightmare, as you are turned away from motels, parks, attractions, and beaches. The moral? Make plans. Several books are available listing establishments that accept pets. (Look in your library or book store.) Call ahead to attractions to see if they have arrangements for pets.

The number of establishments that accept pets decreases yearly. You can thank dog owners who seem to think

their little "Rascal" is above the law, owners who let Rascal defecate on sidewalks, beaches, and playgrounds, bark himself hoarse in the motel room, and leave behind wet spots on the carpet and chew marks on the chairs.

Luckily some places still remain where pets are welcome. Schedule several stops in places your Jack Russell can enjoy. If you are driving, bring a long retractable lead so your dog can stretch its legs safely every few hours along the way. Keep an eye out for little nature excursions, which are wonderful for refreshing both dog and owner. But always do so with a cautious eye; never risk your or your dog's safety by stopping in totally desolate locales, no matter how breathtaking the view.

The Doggy Seat Belt

Ideally your JRT should always ride with the equivalent of a doggy seat belt: the cage. Not only can a cage help to prevent accidents by keeping your dog from using your lap as a trampoline, but, if an accident does happen, a cage can save your dog's life. A cage with a padlocked door can also be useful when you need to leave the dog in the car with the windows down.

Airplane Trips

Although car trips are the most common mode of travel for dogs, sometimes an airplane trip is required (note that dogs are not allowed on trains). Small dogs are often able to ride in the passenger cabin of an airplane, if their cage can fit under the seat. Always opt for this choice if available. When making reservations ask what type of cage you must have.

If you must ship a dog by itself, it is better to ship "counter to counter" than as regular air cargo, and note the following:
• Make sure the cage is secure, and for good measure put an elastic "bungee" band around the cage door.

- Don't feed your dog before traveling. The cage should have a small dish that can be attached to the door. The night before the trip fill it with water and freeze it; as it melts during the flight, the dog will have water that otherwise would have spilled out during the loading process.
- Include a large chewbone to occupy your jet-setter.
- Be sure to line the cage with soft, absorbent material, preferably something that can be thrown away if soiled.
- Although air compartments are heated, they are not air-conditioned, and in hot weather dogs have been known to overheat while the plane was still on the runway. Never ship in the heat of day.

The cage is the Jack Russell's seat belt, preferably belted into place.

Spending the Night Away from Home

Whether you will be spending your nights at a motel, campground, or even a friend's home, always have your dog on its very best behavior. Ask beforehand if it will be OK for you to bring your Jack Russell. Have your dog clean and parasite free. Do not allow your dog to run helter-skelter through the homes of friends. Bring your dog's own clean blanket or bed, or better yet, its cage. Your JRT will appreciate the familiar place to sleep, and your friends and motel owners will breathe sighs of relief. Even though your dog may be accustomed to sleeping on furniture at home, a proper canine guest stays on the floor when visiting. Walk and walk your dog (and clean up after it) to make sure no accidents occur inside. If they do, clean them immediately. Don't leave any surprises for your hosts! Changes in water or food, or simply stress can often result in diarrhea, so be particularly attentive to taking your dog out often. *Never, never* leave your dog unattended in a strange place. The dog's perception is that you have left and forgotten it; it either barks or tries to dig its way out through the doors and windows in an effort to find you, or becomes upset and relieves itself on the carpet. Always remember that anyone who allows your dog to spend the night is doing so with a certain amount of trepidation; make sure your JRT is so well behaved that you are both invited back.

The JRT's Travel Case

Your JRT should have its own travel case that should include:
- first aid kit
- heartworm preventative and any other medications, especially antidiarrhea medication
- food and water bowls
- some dog biscuits and chewies
- flea spray
- flea comb and brush
- bedding
- short and long leashes
- sweater for cold weather
- flashlight for night walks
- plastic baggies or other poop disposal means

"Are we ready to go yet?"

- moist towelettes, paper towels, and self-rinse shampoo
- food (the type the dog is used to eating, to avoid stomach upsets)
- dog tags, including license tags and a tag indicating where you could be reached while on your trip, or including the address of someone you know will be at home
- recent color photo in case your JRT somehow gets lost
- health and rabies certificates
- bottled water or water from home (many dogs are very sensitive to changes in water and can develop diarrhea)

With a little foresight you may find your Jack Russell to be the most entertaining and enjoyable travel companion you could invite along. And don't be surprised if you find your dog nestled in your suitcase among your packed clothes!

Even if the only trip you take with your JRT is around the block, please, for the sake of dog ownership in the future, maintain the same high standards that you would if traveling:

This JRT is free to roam within the confines of a big fenced-in yard.

- Always clean up after your dog. Carry a little plastic bag for disposal later.
- Don't let your dog run loose where it could bother picnickers, bicyclists, joggers, or children.
- Never let your dog bark unchecked.
- Never let your dog jump up on people.
- Never take a chance of your dog biting anybody.
- Don't allow your JRT to lunge at other dogs.

Boarding

Sometimes you must leave your dog behind when you travel. Ask friends or your veterinarian for boarding kennel recommendations. The ideal kennel will be approved by the American Boarding Kennel Association, have climate-controlled accommodations, and will keep your JRT either indoors or in a combination indoor/outdoor run. Make an unannounced visit to the kennel and ask to see the facilities. While you can't expect spotlessness and a perfumy atmosphere, most runs should be clean and the odor should not be overpowering. All dogs should have clean water and at least some bedding. Good kennels will require proof of immunizations, and an incoming check for fleas. They will allow you to bring toys and bedding, and will administer prescribed medication. Strange dogs should not be allowed to mingle, and the entire kennel area should be fenced.

Your dog may be more comfortable if an experienced pet-sitter or responsible friend comes to your home and feeds and exercises your dog regularly. This works best if you have a doggy door. The kid next door is seldom a good choice for this important responsibility. It is too easy for the dog to slip out the door, or for signs of illness to go unnoticed, unless the sitter is an experienced dog person.

Whatever means you choose, always leave emergency numbers and your veterinarian's name. Make arrangements with your veterinarian to treat your dog for any problems that may arise. This means leaving a written agreement stating that you give permission for treatment and accept responsibility for charges.

Little Dog Lost

Never leave your dog in a place where it would be vulnerable to a Jack Russell hijack, and never be complacent about your dog's absence. If your JRT escapes or gets lost, you must act quickly in order to ensure its safe return. Start your search at the very worst place you could imagine it going, usually the nearest highway. Don't drive recklessly and endanger your own dog's life should it run across the road. If you still can't find your pet, get pictures of your dog and go door to door; ask any workers or delivery persons in the area. Search for any burrows that your JRT may be exploring. Some dogs have been lost for days only to be found underground with a cornered animal. Call the local animal control, police department, and veterinarians. If your dog is tattooed (see Useful Addresses, page 98), contact the tattoo registry. Make up *large* posters with a picture of a JRT. Take out an ad in the local paper. Mention a reward, but do not specify an amount.

Never give anyone reward money before seeing your dog. There are a number of scams involving answering lost dog ads, many asking for money for shipping the dog back to you from a distance or for paying vet bills, when very often these people have not really found your dog. If your dog is tattooed, you can have the person read the tattoo to you in order to positively identify it.

Tattooing

Even license tags cannot always ensure your dog's return, because they must be on the dog to be effective. Tattooing your social security number or your dog's registration number on the inside of its thigh provides a permanent means of identification; these numbers can be registered with one of the several lost pet recovery agencies. Microchips are now available that are placed under the dog's skin with a simple injection. They contain information about the dog and cannot be removed, but require a special scanner (owned by most animal shelters) to be read (see Useful Addresses, page 98). You may wish to discuss this option with your veterinarian or local breeders.

The Friend of a Lifetime

You have a lifetime of experiences to share with your new Jack Russell terrier. The remainder of your dog's life will be spent under your care and guidance. Your life may change dramatically in the years to come: marriage, divorce, new baby, new home—for better or worse, your dog will still depend on you and still love you. Always remember the promise you made to yourself and your future puppy before you made the commitment to share your life: to keep your interest in your dog and care for it every day of its life with as much love and enthusiasm as you did the first day it arrived home.

Jack Russell Terriers Can Be Trained

Part of the current appeal of the JRT has arisen from its frequent television appearances, leading to the perception that JRTs are easy to train. Not necessarily! Some of the most talented JRT stars were actually intolerable as pets and were initially obedience school dropouts! In the hands of professional dog trainers, such canine delinquents, always in motion and perpetually inquisitive, make the best show biz candidates. This is because it is easier to train a dog *when* to do something than it is to train one *how* to do something.

Dog training methods have changed little through the years—but they should have. Traditional dog training methods based on force are the least successful and most widespread. The problem with training by force is that it relies upon punishment as a means of telling the dog what *not* to do, but it is seldom successful in telling the dog what it *should* do.

Food for Thought

Many years ago the idea was perpetuated that dogs should never be trained with food. Yet professional animal trainers and animal learning scientists all knew that food training produced excellent results because food tells the animal what behaviors are correct. Only recently has food-motivated training become accepted in training the family dog, and owners are finding that dogs learn faster, mind more reliably, work more eagerly, and have a more trusting dog-owner relationship.

JRTs often have a "What's in it for me?" attitude, and food provides them with a satisfactory answer. At first food is used to guide the dog by the nose until it is in the desired position, and then rewarding it. After the dog knows what is expected, the food is held out of sight and only given to the dog when it has performed correctly. Ultimately, the dog is weaned from getting a food reward each time, but still gets one every once in a while. Such a random payoff schedule has been shown to be very effective in both animals and humans (as in slot machine payoffs!).

The idea of bribing our dogs with food runs counter to the idealized pic-

The well-trained dog gains confidence and enjoys life more because it is trusted to behave in all situations. Training your Jack Russell is the best gift you can give it.

ture of Lassie obeying out of pure goodness and love. But the real Lassie, of course, was performing for food rewards. Dog owners have been told for years that the dog should work for praise alone, but praise alone is not really a terribly strong motivator for most dogs, and even worse for most JRTs. Praise can become a stronger motivator by always praising immediately before the food reward is given. In this way it becomes a secondary reinforcer, much as a gold star on a child's schoolwork gains reinforcing value because it has been paired with other positive reinforcement. Eventually, the dog can be weaned from the food and will come to work in large part for praise, but food should still be given as a reward intermittently.

Jack Russell terriers will happily come when called if you make it worth their while.

Terrier Training Tips

JRTs are highly intelligent but can be a handful unless trained properly. To live in peace with your JRT use the same training techniques that the professionals use. Remember the following rules of terrier training:

• **Guide, don't force:** JRTs want to please you but they also want to please themselves. They are especially poor candidates for force training, and don't take well to being bullied into submission. Tough, domineering training techniques are more likely to bring out the stubborn streak in a JRT. In a battle of the wills, the JRT will usually win.

• **Correct, don't punish:** Such methods as striking, shaking, choking and even hanging have been touted by some (stupid) trainers. Do not try them! They are extremely dangerous, counterproductive, and cruel. They have no place in the training of a beloved family member—plus, they don't work. Remember, JRTs are bred to continue on in the face of adversity.

• **Correct and be done with it:** Owners sometimes try to make this "a correction the dog will remember" by ignoring the dog for the rest of the day. The dog may indeed remember that its owner ignored it, but it will not remember why. The dog can only relate its present behavior to your actions.

• **You get what you ask for:** Dogs repeat actions that bring them rewards, whether you intend for them to or not. Feeding your JRT to make it be quiet might work momentarily, but in the long run you will end up with a noisier dog, because your JRT learns that barking brings food. Make sure you reward only those behaviors you want to see more often.

• **Mean what you say:** Sometimes a Jack Russell can be awfully cute when it misbehaves, or sometimes your hands are full, and sometimes you just aren't sure what you want from your dog. But lapses in consistency are ultimately unfair to the dog. If you feed your JRT from the table because it begs "just this one time," you have taught it that while begging may not always result in a handout, you never know, it just might pay off tonight. In other words, you have taught your dog to beg.

• **Say what you mean:** Your JRT takes its commands literally. If you have taught that *"Down"* means to lie down, then what must the dog think when you yell *"Down"* to tell it to get off the sofa where it was already lying down? Or *"Sit down"* when you mean *"Sit?"* If *"Stay"* means not to move until given a release word, and you say *"Stay here"* as you leave the house for work, do you really want your dog to sit by the door all day until you get home?

• **Train before meals:** Your JRT will work better if its stomach is not full, and will be more responsive to food rewards. Never try to train a sleepy, tired, or hot JRT.

• **Happy endings:** Begin and end each training session with something the dog can do well. And keep sessions short and fun—no longer than 10 to 15 minutes. Dogs have short attention spans and you will notice that after about 15 minutes their performance will begin to suffer unless a lot of play is involved. To continue to train a tired or bored dog will result in the training of bad habits, resentment in the dog, and frustration for the trainer.

Some small dog training aids: a section of PVC pipe with a leash strung through it, and a lightweight backscratcher or stick.

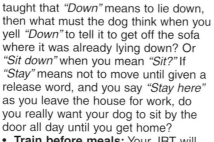

The correct placement of the choke collar is with the long end (to which the lead is attached) coming over the top of the dog's head from the dog's left to right side.

Especially when training a young puppy, or when you only have one or two different exercises to practice, quit while you are ahead! Keep your JRT wanting more, and you will have a happy, willing, obedience partner.

• **Name, command, action!** The first ingredient in any command is your dog's name. You probably spend a good deal of your day talking, with very few words intended as commands for your dog. So warn your terrier that this talk is directed toward it.

Many trainers make the mistake of saying the command word *at the same time* that they are placing the dog into position. *This is incorrect.* The command comes immediately *before* the desired action or position. The crux of training is anticipation: The dog comes to anticipate that, after hearing a command, it will be induced to perform some action, and it will eventually perform this action without further assistance from you. On the other hand, when the command and action come at the same time, not only does the dog tend to pay more attention to your action of placing it in position, and less attention to the command word, but the command word loses its predictive value for the dog. Remember: Name, command, action, reward!

• **Once is enough:** Repeating a command over and over, or shouting it louder and louder, never helped anyone, dog or human, understand what is expected of them. Your JRT is not hard of hearing.

• **Think like a dog:** Dogs live in the present; if you punish them they can only assume it is for their behavior at the time of punishment. So if you discover a mess, and drag your dog to it from its nap in the other room, and scold, the impression to the dog will be that either it is being scolded for napping, or that its owner is mentally unstable. In many ways dogs are like young children; they act to gratify themselves, and they often do so without thinking ahead to consequences. But, unlike young children, dogs cannot understand human language (except for those words you teach them), so you cannot explain to them that their actions of five minutes earlier were bad. Remember, timing is everything in a correction. If you discover your dog in the process of having an "accident," and snatch the dog up and deposit it outside, and then yell *"No,"* your dog can only conclude that you have yelled *"No"* to it for eliminating outside. Correct timing would be *"No,"* quickly take the dog outside, and then reward it once it eliminates outside. In this way you have corrected the dog's undesired behavior and helped the dog understand desired behavior.

• **The best laid plans:** Finally, nothing will ever go just as perfectly as it seems to in all of the training instructions but, although there may be setbacks, you can train your dog, as long as you remember to be consistent, firm, gentle, realistic, and most of all, patient.

Training Equipment

Equipment for training should include a six-foot (1.8 m) and a 20-foot (6 m) lightweight lead. For puppies it is convenient to use one of the lightweight adjustable size show leads. Some JRTs can be trained with a buckle collar, but a choke collar is also an acceptable choice as long as you know how to use it correctly.

A choke collar is not for choking! The proper way to administer a correction with a choke collar is with a gentle snap, then immediate release. If you think the point of the correction is to startle the dog by the sound of the chain links moving, rather than to choke or in any way hurt your dog, you will be correcting with the right level of force. The choke collar is placed on the dog so that the ring with the lead attached comes up around the left side of the dog's neck, and through the other ring. If put on backwards, it will not release itself after being tightened (since you will be on the right side of your dog for most training). The choke collar should *never* be left on your Jack Russell after a training sessions; there are too many tragic cases where a choke collar really did earn its name after being snagged on a fence, bush, or even a playmate's tooth. Allowing a dog to run around wearing a choke collar is like allowing a child to run around wearing a hangman's noose.

A Dog's-Eye View

How can you train a dog if you can't communicate with it? And how do you communicate with a member of another species when you live in two very different sensory worlds? In order to see eye-to-eye with your JRT, you need to understand the world it lives in and the way it talks.

Like their wolf ancestors, Jack Russells depend upon facial expressions and body language in social interactions:
• A yawn is often a sign of nervousness.
• Drooling and panting can indicate extreme nervousness (or carsickness).
• The combination of a wagging tail, lowered head, and exposed teeth upon greeting is a sign of submission.
• The combination of a lowered body,

Extreme submissive pose.

The classic "play-bow" position.

The nervous dog will pant, drool, and shake, as well as hold its ears back.

Threatening position.

wagging tucked tail, urination, and perhaps even rolling over is a sign of extreme submission.

• The combination of exposed teeth, a high, rigidly held tail, raised hackles, very upright posture, stiff-legged gait, direct stare, forward raised ears, and perhaps leg lifting to urinate indicates very dominant, possibly threatening behavior.

• The combination of a wagging tail, front legs and elbows on the ground, and rear in the air, with or without vocalizations is the classic "play-bow" position, and is an invitation for a game.

Your JRT not only speaks a different language than you do, but it lives in a different sensory world.

• **Olfaction:** The dog's scenting ability is so vastly superior to ours that it is as though we were blind in comparison. The dog can seek out hidden objects and animals, follow a trail for miles, and distinguish between individuals by scent. The JRT is a particularly adept scenter, and you would do well to trust its nose.

• **Taste:** Dogs also have a well-developed sense of taste, and have most of the same taste receptors that we do. Research has shown that they prefer meat (not exactly earth-shaking news!), and while there are many individual differences, the average dog prefers beef, pork, lamb, chicken, and horsemeat, in that order. Of course, JRTs sometimes seem to prefer anything in reach!

Dogs have sugar receptors similar to ours, which explains why many have a sweet tooth. But their perception of artificial sweeteners is not like ours, and they seem to taste bitter to them.

• **Vision:** No dogs see the world with as much detail or color as do humans. The dog's sense of color is similar to that of what is commonly called a "color-blind" person, which is not really blind to color at all. That is, they confuse similar shades of yellow-green,

The acute sensory organs of the Jack Russell terrier enable it to hear higher frequencies and see in dimmer light than can humans, and especially, to smell an entire world of enticing odors.

yellow, orange, and red, but can readily see and discriminate blue, indigo, and violet from all other colors and each other.

The dog's eye is superior when it comes to seeing in very dim light. The eyeshine you may see from your dog's eyes at night is from a reflective structure (the tapetum lucidum) that serves to increase its ability to see in very dim light, and the dog has a greater proportion of the type of retinal cells (rods) that are highly sensitive to dim light than humans have. Your JRT is very much at home in the near dark.

• **Hearing:** Dogs can hear much higher tones than can humans, and so can be irritated by high hums from your TV or from those ultrasonic flea collars. The high-pitched "dog whistles" so popular years ago emit a tone higher than humans can hear, but well within the dog's range. Dogs need to be trained to respond to these whistles just as they would any other command or signal. A problem is that owners can't tell when the whistle malfunctions.

Ultrasonic training devices now available emit a high-frequency sound inaudible to us, but irritating and distracting to dogs. They can be a useful training aid for disrupting unwanted behavior, but only if accompanied by rewarding the dog for correct behavior.

• **Pain:** Many people erroneously believe that animals cannot feel pain, but common sense and scientific research indicate that dogs and other animals have a well-developed sense of pain. Many dogs are amazingly stoic, however, and their ability to deal with pain is not totally understood at present. Because a dog may not be able to express that it is in

HOW-TO:
Basic Commands

It's never too early or too late to start the education of your Jack Russell terrier. With a very young JRT, train for short time periods. By the time your JRT pup (here named "Wolfman") reaches six months of age, it should be familiar with several necessary commands.

Following are the most important commands your JRT should know:

Watch Me

A common problem when training any dog is that the dog's attention is elsewhere. You can teach your dog to pay attention to you by teaching it the *watch me* command. Say "Wolfman, *watch me*," and when he looks in your direction, give him a treat or other reward. Gradually require the dog to look at you for longer and longer periods before rewarding it.

Use food to guide your dog's head backwards and slightly up. If you position its rear end next to a wall, it will have to sit in order to reach the treat.

54

Make coming on command fun (and tasty)!

Teach *watch me* before going on to the other commands.

Tip: Teach stationary exer-cises on a tabletop or other raised sur-face. This allows you to have eye contact with your dog and gives you a bet-ter vantage from which to help your dog learn.

Sit

Because JRTs are already close to the ground, many of them virtually teach themselves to sit as a means of being more comfortable while looking up at you. But you can hasten the process by holding a tidbit above your puppy's eye level, saying "Wolfman, *sit*," and then moving the tidbit toward your pup until it is slightly behind and above his eyes. You may have to keep a hand on his rump to prevent him from jumping up. When the puppy begins to look up and bend his hind legs, praise, then offer the tidbit. Repeat this, requiring the dog to bend his legs more and more until he must be sitting before receiving praise.

Tip: To train your dog at your feet, extend your arm length with a back scratcher with

which to guide and even pet your dog without having to bend over.

Stay

A dangerous habit of many dogs is to bolt through open doors, whether they are in the house or car. Teach your dog to sit and stay until given the release signal before walking through the front door or exiting your car.

Have your dog sit, then say *"Stay"* in a soothing voice. (For commands in which the dog is not supposed to move, don't precede the command with the dog's name.) If your JRT attempts to get up or lie down, gently but instantly place it back into position. After the first few tries you'll quickly under-stand how a Jack-in-the-Box got its name, but eventually your Jack Russell will forget and leave its rear on the ground for a few seconds. Reward! Then work up to a few seconds, give a release word (*"OK!"*), praise, and give a tid-bit. Next, step out (starting with your right foot) and turn to stand directly in front of your dog while it stays. Work up to longer times, but don't ask a young puppy to stay longer than 30 seconds. The object is not to push your dog to the limit, but to let it succeed. To do this you must be very patient, and you must increase your times and distances in very small increments. Finally, practice with the dog on lead by the front door or in the car. For a reward, take him for a walk!

Tip: Don't stare at your dog during the *stay*, as this is perceived by the dog as a threat and often intimidates it so that it squirms out of position or creeps to you submissively.

Once the sit is mastered, use food to lure your dog to the ground. You may have to keep a hand on its rump to prevent it from getting up.

Come

Coming on command is more than a cute trick—it could save your dog's life. Your puppy probably already knows how to come; after all, it comes when it sees you with the food bowl, or perhaps with the leash or a favorite toy. You may have even used the word *"Come"* to get its attention then. If so, you have a head start. You want your puppy to respond to "Wolfman, *come*" with the same enthusiasm as though you were setting down his supper; in other words, *"Come"* should always be associated with good things.

Tip: Never have your dog come to you and then scold it for something it has done. In the dog's mind it is being scolded for coming, not for any earlier misdeed.

Most trainers only teach *"Come"* from a sitting position, but in real life the dog is seldom sitting when you want it to come. With the pup on lead, command "Wolfman, *come!*" enthusiastically, and back or run away, luring him with the tidbit. When he reaches you, praise and reward him. When he seems to have the idea, attach a longer line to him, allow him to meander about, and in the midst of his investigations, call, run backwards, and reward. Eventually you can just stand still when you call. You should ultimately practice (on lead) in the presence of distractions, such as other leashed dogs, unfamiliar people, cats, and cars.

Tip: Have your JRT sit in front of you before getting the tidbit in order to prevent the annoying habit some dogs have of dancing around just beyond your reach.

Down

When you need your JRT to stay in one place for a long time it is best for it to be left in a *down/stay*. Begin teaching the *down* command with the dog in the sitting position. Command "Wolfman, *down,*" then show him a tidbit and move it below his nose toward the ground. If he reaches down to get it, give it to him. Repeat, requiring him to reach further down (without lifting his rear from the ground) until he has to lower his elbows to the ground. Never try to cram your dog into the *down* position, which can scare a submissive dog and cause a dominant dog to resist.

Tip: Teach *down* on a table-top, curb edge, or at the head of the stairs, anywhere the dog is slightly elevated so you can get the tidbit below the dog's chin at floor level.

Practice the *down/stay* just as you did the *sit/stay*. Eventually work up to three minutes.

Tip: Occasionally have your dog lie in a *down/stay* on its side and groom and examine it. Give it a treat for remaining calm. This is a useful exercise for grooming or veterinary attention. You can even teach a separate command that means "lie on your side" rather than in the traditional "sphinx" position.

pain, you must be alert to changes in your dog's demeanor. A stiff gait, low head carriage, reluctance to get up, irritability, dilated pupils, whining, or limping are all indications that your dog is in pain.

Electric shock collars produce a mild electrical stimulation (produced from flashlight batteries) that is probably more startling and irritating than it is painful to dogs. Used correctly, they can be a useful tool for teaching obedience at a distance. Most people don't know how to use them properly, however, and they are not recommended except under an experienced trainer's guidance. Punishment without instruction can cause worse behavioral problems.

Teaching Your JRT to Heel

Your pup should be acquainted with a lightweight leash by the time it has learned *come*. Still, walking alongside of you on lead is a new experience for a youngster, and many will freeze in their tracks once they discover their freedom is being violated. In this case,

Don't jerk your dog into the heel position. Guide it with food. The proper heel position is on your left side, with the dog's neck in line with your leg.

do not simply drag the pup along, but coax it with food. When the puppy follows you, praise and reward. The pup thus comes to realize that following you while walking on lead pays off.

Most JRTs have a tendency to forge ahead, pulling their hapless owners behind them, zigzagging from bush to fencepost. Although at times this may be acceptable to you, at other times it will be annoying and perhaps even dangerous. Even if you have no intention of teaching a perfect competition *heel*, you need to teach it as a way of letting your JRT know it is your turn to be the leader.

Tip: A leash that comes from several feet overhead has virtually no guiding ability whatsoever. You need a lower pivot point for the leash in relation to the dog, and you can achieve this by what is called a "solid leash." This is simply a hollow, light tube, such as PVC pipe, about 3 feet (91 cm) long, through which you string your leash. To prevent your dog from sitting or lying down, loop part of your regular leash around its belly and hold onto that part, so you have a convenient "handle."

Using the solid leash, have your JRT sit in the *heel* position; that is, on your left side with its neck next to and parallel with your leg. Say "Wolfman, *heel*" and step off with your left foot first. (Remember that you stepped off on your right foot when you left your dog on a *stay*. If you are consistent, the foot that moves first will provide an eye-level cue for your little dog.) During your first few practice sessions you will keep him on a short lead, holding him in *heel* position, and of course praising him. The traditional method of letting the dog lunge to the end of the lead and then snapping it back is unfair if you haven't shown the dog what is expected of him at first. Instead, after a few sessions of showing the dog the *heel* position, give him a little more loose lead and use a tidbit to guide him into correct position. If your JRT still forges ahead after you have shown him what is expected, pull him back to position with a quick gentle tug, then release, of the lead.

If, after a few days' practice, your dog still seems oblivious to your efforts, then turn unexpectedly several times. This will result in a jerk to your dog, but don't feel too guilty—you tried to show him the right path. Give your dog a chance to *heel* in position before resorting to another unexpected turn. Your dog will learn that you can be unpredictable, and if it wants to avoid the jerk, it had better keep an eye on you and remain by your side. Be forewarned that if you use this correction too often, you will have an unhappy heeler that continually lags behind you in order to keep you in its line of sight.

Tip: Keep up a pace that requires your JRT to walk fairly briskly; too slow a pace gives dogs time to sniff, look all around and in general become distracted; a brisk pace will focus the dog's attention upon you and generally aid training.

As you progress you will want to add some right, left, and about-faces, and walk at all different speeds. Then practice in different areas (still always on-lead) and around different distractions. You can teach your JRT to sit every time you stop. Vary your routine to combat boredom, and keep training sessions short. Be sure to give the *OK* command before allowing your dog to sniff, forge, and meander on lead.

Tricks and Treats

The only problem with basic obedience skills is that they don't exactly astound your friends. For that you need something flashy, some incredible feat of intelligence and dexterity: a dog trick. Try the standards: *roll over, play dead, catch, sit up, speak.* All are easy to teach with the help of the

Unusually intelligent, Jack Russells can learn to do just about anything—for the price of a tidbit!

same obedience concepts outlined in the training section. Teach *roll over* by giving the command when the dog is already on its back, then guide it the rest of the way over with a treat. Teach speak by saying *"Speak"* when it appears your JRT is about to bark. Teach *catch* by throwing a tidbit or other item your dog wants; when it lands on the ground, snatch it up before your dog can. Your dog will quickly figure out the only way to get it is to grab it in midair! If your dog can physically do it, you can teach it when to do it. The success of JRTs as animal actors shows how adept they are at learning tricks of all sorts.

JRT Nutrition

Fueling Your Jack Russell Terrier

"You are what you eat" is just as true for dogs as it is for people. Because your JRT can't go shopping for its dinner, it "will be what you feed it," so you have total responsibility for feeding your dog a high-quality balanced diet that will enable it to live a long and active life. Dog food claims can be conflicting and confusing, but there are some guidelines that you can use when selecting a proper diet for your Jack Russell terrier.

High Octane

Although dogs are members of the order Carnivora ("meateaters"), they are actually omnivorous, meaning their nutritional needs can be met by a diet derived from both animals and plants. Most dogs do have a decided prefer-

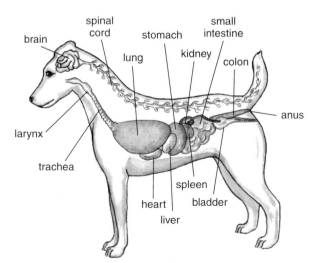

Internal organs of the Jack Russell terrier.

ence for meat over non-meat foods, but a balanced meal will combine both meat and plant-based nutrients:

• **Dry food** (containing about 10 percent moisture) is the most popular, economical, and healthy, but least palatable form of dog food.

• **Semimoist** foods (with about 30 percent moisture) contain high levels of sugar used as preservatives. They are palatable and convenient, and very handy for traveling. Semimoist foods are not a very good nutritional choice, and can result in excessive water consumption, leading to excessive urination. Pay no attention to their meat-like shapes; they all start out as a powder and are formed to look like meat chunks or ground beef.

• **Canned food** has a high moisture content (about 75 percent), which helps to make them tasty, but it also makes them comparatively expensive, since you are in essence buying water. A steady diet of canned food would not provide the chewing necessary to maintain dental health. In addition, a high meat content tends to increase levels of dental plaque. Supplementation with chew sticks, nylon bones, and dog biscuits can provide the necessary chewing action. Most people mix canned and dry food.

• **Dog biscuits** provide excellent chewing action, and some of the better varieties provide complete nutrition. They are convenient for snacks and travel.

Nutrient Levels

The Association of American Feed Control Officials (AAFCO) has recommended minimal nutrient levels for dogs based upon controlled feeding studies. Unless you are a nutritionist, the chances of your cooking up a homemade diet that meets these exacting standards is remote so the first rule is to select a food that states on the label not only that it meets the requirements set by the AAFCO, but also has been tested in *feeding trials*. You should also realize that when you add table scraps and other entice-ments, you are disrupting the balance of the diet.

Feed a high-quality food from a name-brand company. Dog owners tend to be one of three types when it comes to feeding their dogs: the first tries to save money by feeding dog food made from sawdust and corn-cobs, and then wonders why the dog has to eat so much of it; the other extreme chooses a food because it costs the most and is made from bee pollen, llama milk, and caviar yolk (and of course, no preservatives) and then wonders why the food is rancid half the time and their dog is a blimp; and the third type buys a high-quality food from a recognized source that has proven their food through actual feed-ing trials. Avoid food that has been sit-ting on the shelf for long periods, or that has holes in the bag or grease that has seeped through the bag.

Finally, find a food that your terrier enjoys. Mealtime is a highlight of a dog's day. Although a dog will eventu-ally eat even the most unsavory of dog food if given no choice, it hardly seems fair to deprive your family member of one of life's simple and, for a dog, most important, pleasures.

A word of caution: Dogs will often seem to prefer a new food when it is first offered, but this may simply be due to its novelty. Only after you buy a six-month supply of this alleged canine ambrosia will you discover it was just a passing fancy—one more reason you should never buy a lot of dog food at once.

Dog food now comes in a dizzying array of types, flavors, and specialties.

When comparing food labels, keep in mind that differences in moisture content make it difficult to make direct comparisons between the guaranteed analyses in various forms of food. The components that vary most from one brand of food to another are protein and fat percentages.

Protein: Many high-quality foods boast of being high in protein, and with good reason. Protein provides the nec-essary building blocks for growth and maintenance of bones, muscle, and coat, and in the production of infection fighting antibodies. Meat-derived pro-tein is more highly digestible than plant-derived protein, and is of higher quality. The quality of protein is as important as the quantity of protein.

Puppies and adolescents need par-ticularly high protein levels in their diets, which is one reason they should be fed a food formulated for their life stage. Older dogs, especially those with kidney problems, should be fed lower levels of very high-quality protein. Studies have shown that high-protein diets do not cause kidney failure in older dogs but, if the dog has kidney stress or decompensation, a high-pro-tein diet will do a lot of harm. If your JRT is active throughout the day, or is underweight, you may want to feed it a

The combination of good taste and good nutrition will have your Jack Russell dancing for its dinner.

digestible foods mean less stool volume and fewer gas problems.

You may have to do a little experimenting to find just the right food, but a word of warning: One of the great mysteries of life is why a species, such as the dog, that is known for its lead stomach and preference to eat out of garbage cans, can at the same time develop violently upset stomachs simply from changing from one high-quality dog food to another. But it happens. So when changing foods you should do so gradually, mixing in progressively more and more of the new food each day for several days.

Fill'er Up?

The dog's wild ancestor, the wolf, evolved to survive feast and famine, gorging following a kill but then perhaps waiting several days before another feast. In today's world, dogs can feast daily and without the period of famine can easily become obese.

Very young puppies should be fed three or four times a day, on a regular schedule. Feed them as much as they want to eat in about 15 minutes. From the age of three to six months, pups should be fed three times daily; after that, twice daily. Adult dogs can be fed once a day, but it is actually preferable to feed smaller meals twice a day.

Some people let the dog decide when to eat by leaving food available at all times. If you choose to let the dog "self-feed," monitor its weight to be sure it is not overindulging. Leave only dry food down. Canned food spoils rapidly and becomes both unsavory and unhealthy. If your dog overindulges, you will have to intervene before you have an obese JRT on your hands.

A JRT in proper weight should have ribs that can just be felt when you run your hands along the rib cage. Viewed from above, it should have an hourglass figure. There should be no roll of fat over the withers or rump.

high-quality protein food. Most JRT housedogs will do fine on regular adult foods having protein levels of about 20 percent (dry food percentage).

Fat: Fat is the calorie-rich component of foods, and most dogs prefer the taste of foods with higher fat content. Fat is necessary to good health, aiding in the transport of important vitamins and providing energy. Dogs deficient in fat often have sparse, dry coats. A higher fat content is usually found in puppy foods, while obese dogs or dogs with heart problems should be fed a lower fat food. Many high-protein foods also have a high fat content.

Choose a food that has a protein and fat content best suited for your dog's life stage, adjusting for any weight or health problems (prescription diets formulated for specific health problems are available). Also examine the list of ingredients: A good rule of thumb is that three or four of the first six ingredients should be animal derived. These tend to be more palatable and more highly digestible than plant-based ingredients; more highly

Fat Jacks

If your JRT is overweight, switch to one of the commercially available high-fiber, low-fat and medium-protein diet dog foods that supply about 15 percent fewer calories per pound. It is preferable to feed one of these foods rather than simply feeding less of a high-calorie food. Make sure family members aren't sneaking the dog forbidden tidbits.

Many people find that one of the many pleasures of dog ownership is sharing a special treat with their pet. Rather than giving up this bonding activity, substitute a low-calorie alternative such as rice cakes or carrots, or even a small cube of cooked, chicken breast. Keep the dog out of the kitchen or dining area at food preparation or mealtimes. Schedule a walk immediately following your dinner to get your dog's mind off your leftovers—it will be good for both of you.

If your dog remains overweight, seek your veterinarian's opinion. Heart disease and some endocrine disorders, such as hypothyroidism or Cushing's disease, or the early stages of diabetes, can cause the appearance of obesity and should be ruled out or treated. However, most cases of obesity are simply from eating more calories than are expended. Obesity predisposes dogs to joint injuries and heart problems. The JRT is too fun loving to be burdened by a body of blubber.

Jack Sprats

If you have an underweight dog, try feeding puppy food, adding water, milk, bouillon, or canned food, and heating the food slightly to increase aroma and palatability. Milk will cause many dogs to have diarrhea, so start

Never Feed
• Chicken, pork, lamb, or fish bones. These can be swallowed and their sharp ends can pierce the stomach or intestinal walls.
• Any bone that could be swallowed whole. This could cause choking or intestinal blockage.
• Any cooked bone. Cooked bones tend to break and splinter.
• Raw meat. It could contain salmonella.
• Mineral supplements unless advised to do so by your veterinarian.
• Chocolate. It contains theobromine, which is poisonous to dogs.
• Alcohol. Small dogs can drink fatal amounts quickly.

with only a small amount at first. Try a couple of dog food brands, but if your JRT still won't eat, you may have to employ some tough love. Many picky eaters are created when their owners begin to spice up their food with especially tasty treats. The dog then refuses to eat unless the preferred treat is offered, and finally learns that if it refuses even that proffered treat, another even tastier enticement will be offered. Give your dog a good, tasty meal, but don't succumb to Jack Russell blackmail or you may be a slave to your dog's gastronomical whims for years to come.

Most JRTs are "easy-keepers," meaning they eat readily, are not finicky, and also seem to maintain their weight at an optimal level.

An exception is a sick dog, in which case feeding by hand is warranted. Cat food or meat baby food are both relished by dogs and may entice a dog without an appetite to eat.

Jack Russell Terrier Maintenance

Hair of the Dog

Care of the Jack Russell jacket is simple, especially for the wash-and-wear smooth coat. Weekly brushing with a bristle brush or rubber shedding mitt, and an occasional bath will suffice for the pet. For special occasions, tidying up the few scraggly hairs under the tail, rump, abdomen, and feet is all that is required.

The rough coat, however, needs considerably more care to retain the proper JRT appearance. If left unattended, the coat will grow overly long, soft, and scraggly, and the dog will lose the crisp, neat outline so typical of the JRT. This is especially true of undesirable, overly long or soft coats. But shaving the coat is not the answer. When the hair is cut it exposes the soft undercoat and results in a dog that does not have the proper harsh terrier texture coat. Instead, the coat should be plucked, pulling out the longer dead hairs and allowing new harsh hair to grow back in its place. The hair should be left longer on the muzzle, chest, and legs.

Combing

Before plucking, comb the dog all over. Dead hairs in the comb are a sign that the coat needs attention. Grasp a few long hairs between your thumb and index finger and give a quick yank in the direction of hair growth. This should not be painful for your JRT if the hair is ready to come out. If it doesn't come right out, wait a few days and try again. Brushing some grooming chalk into the

coat beforehand will help you get a better grip on the hair. You can also use a stripping comb to accomplish the job, which will save considerable finger fatigue. To use the stripping comb, place a few hairs between the comb and your thumb and pull in the direction of hair growth with a slight twisting motion. A grooming table will make the process much easier, but you can also use any raised surface covered with a towel to catch the loose hair. The finished JRT should have a neat outline to its body, but without the sculpted look seen in, for example, the wire-haired fox terrier. It should resemble a turned-out hunter rather than a caricature show dog.

Bathing and Shampoos

The harsh texture can also be adversely affected by bathing, although special terrier shampoos are available that will soften the coat less. For the average well-kept JRT, there should be no need to bathe more than once every couple of months.

Your JRT may have other ideas, and after it has perfumed itself with *eau de carrion*, you won't care about coat texture. A supply of rubber gloves comes in handy for such occasions. You will generally get better results with a shampoo made for dogs. Dog skin has a pH of 7.5, while human skin has a pH of 5.5; bathing in a shampoo formulated for the pH of human skin can lead to scaling and irritation in a dog. Most shampoos will kill fleas even if not especially formulated as a flea shampoo, but none has any residual killing action on fleas. No JRT owner should be without one of the shampoos that requires no water or rinsing. These are wonderful for puppies, spot-baths, emergencies, and bathing when time does not permit.

These are therapeutic shampoos for various skin problems:
• for dry scaly skin—moisturizing shampoos
• for excessive scale and dandruff—antiseborrheic shampoos
• for damaged skin—antimicrobials
• for itchy skin—oatmeal-based antipruritics

Even the most devoted of owners seldom look forward to bathtime. Unfortunately, most owners train their dogs to hate baths through improper early bath training. They put off giving a bath and, when they do, they figure that by making it a thorough bath the results will somehow last longer. The secret is to give lots of tiny baths, so tiny the puppy doesn't have a chance to get upset. Rinse (don't even wash) one leg today, an ear tomorrow, and so on. Be firm, soothing, and playful.

A sink or bathtub with a hand-held spray is most convenient. Hold the sprayer against the dog's skin and the dog will not be bothered as much as it would if the spray came from a distance. Use water of a temperature that would be comfortable for you to bathe in, and be sure to keep some running on your own hand in order to monitor any temperature changes. A fractious terrier could inadvertently hit a faucet knob and cause itself (or you) to be scalded. If you keep one hand on your dog's neck or ear, it is less likely to splatter you with a wet dog shake.

Wet your dog down working forward from the rear. Once soaked, use your hand or a soft brush to work in the shampoo (it will go a lot further and be easier to apply if you first mix the shampoo with warm water). Pay spe-cial attention to the oily area around the ear base, but avoid getting water in the dog's ears by plugging them with cotton. Rinse thoroughly, this time working from the head back. Don't use a cream rinse, which would soften the coat.

Shedding

Both coat types shed. Shedding is controlled not by exposure to warmer temperatures, but by exposure to longer periods of light. Thus, indoor dogs that are exposed to artificial light tend to shed somewhat all year.

For other coat problems, note the following:
• Wet or muddy hair can be dried and cleaned by sprinkling on a liberal amount of cornstarch, rubbing it in, and brushing it out.
• Pine tar can be loosened with hair spray.
• Other tar can be worked out with vegetable oil followed by dishwashing detergent.
• Chewing gum can be eased out by first applying ice.
• Skunk odor can be partially washed away with tomato juice. First shampoo, then leave juice on for 15 minutes.

Beauty Is Skin Deep

Your JRT's good looks depend in part upon a healthy coat, but a healthy coat is impossible without healthy skin. Skin problems in all dogs are the most common problems seen by veterinari-ans, and the most common of all skin problems is *flea allergy dermatitis (FAD)*. Itchy, crusted bumps with hair loss in the region around the rump, especially at the base of the tail, results from a flea bite (actually, the flea's saliva) anywhere on the dog's body.

Besides FAD, dogs can have allergic reactions to pollens or other inhaled allergens. Allergies to weeds can man-ifest themselves between the dog's

Whether its coat is smooth, broken, or rough, the JRT should have a sleek outline.

toes. Food allergies can also occur, but are uncommon.

Pyoderma, with pus-filled bumps and crusting, is another common skin disease. *Impetigo* is characterized by such bumps and crusting most often in the groin area of puppies. Both are treated with antibiotics and antibacterial shampoos.

A reddened moist itchy spot that suddenly appears is most likely a "hot spot," which arises from an itch-scratch-chew cycle resulting most commonly from fleas or flea allergy. Clip the surrounding hair, wash the area with an oatmeal-based shampoo, and prevent the dog from further chewing. Use an Elizabethan collar (available from your veterinarian or you can fashion one from a plastic pail), or

an anti-chew preparation such as Bitter Apple (available from most pet stores). Your veterinarian can also prescribe antiinflammatory medication.

In *seborrhea,* there may be excessive dandruff or greasiness, often with excessive ear wax and a rancid odor. Treatment is with antiseborrheic shampoos or diet change.

Hair may be lost in a bilaterally symmetric pattern, without itching, due to hypothyroidism, Cushing's syndrome, or testicular tumors. Consult your veterinarian.

Ticks, Fleas, and JRTs

Ticks

Ticks can carry Rocky Mountain spotted fever, tick paralysis, Lyme disease, and most commonly, "tick fever" (erlichiosis), all potentially fatal diseases. They most often burrow in around the ears, head, neck, and feet. Use a tissue or tweezers to remove ticks, since some diseases can be transmitted to humans. Grasp the tick as close to the skin as possible, and pull slowly and steadily, trying not to leave the head in the dog. Clean the site with alcohol. Often a bump will remain after the tick is removed, even if you got the head. It will go away with time.

Fleas

Look for fleas and their evidence around the chest, belly, and genital areas. Fleas leave behind a black pepper-like substance (actually flea feces) that turns red upon getting wet.

A handy flea detection aid, as well as the safest flea control product, is the flea comb—a comb with such finely spaced teeth that it catches fleas between them. Have a cup of alcohol handy for disposing of the fleas. A cotton ball soaked in alcohol and applied to a flea on the dog will also kill the fleas.

Any flea control program must be undertaken with care, because overzealous and uninformed efforts can lead to the death of pets as well as pests.

Flea control products are categorized as organics, natural pesticides, cholinesterase inhibitors, insect growth regulators, and systemics. Incidentally, ultrasonic flea-repelling collars have been shown to be both ineffective on fleas and irritating to dogs. Scientific studies have also shown that feeding dogs brewer's yeast or garlic, as has been advocated for years by many dog owners, is ineffective against fleas. However, many owners swear it works and it certainly does no harm.

Organics (such as d-limonene) break down the outer shell of the flea and cause it to die from dehydration. They are safe, but slow acting and have no residual action. Diatomaceous earth also acts on this same principle; some researchers have expressed concern that breathing its dust (especially that of the more finely ground pool grade) can be dangerous to dogs, however, a special concern when dealing with a digging dog.

Natural pesticides (such as pyrethrin, permethrin, rotenone) are relatively safe and kill fleas quickly, but have a very short residual action. They do not remain in the dog's system and so can be used frequently.

Cholinesterase inhibitors (Dursban, Diazinon, malathion, Sevin, Carbaryl) act on the nervous systems of fleas, dogs, and humans. They are used in yard sprays, some dog sprays and dips, flea collars, and systemics. They kill effectively and have fairly good residual action but they can poison the dog if overused, and should never be used on puppies or sick dogs.

The **systemics** (Pro-Spot, Spotton) are cholinesterase inhibitors that are applied to the dog's skin for absorption

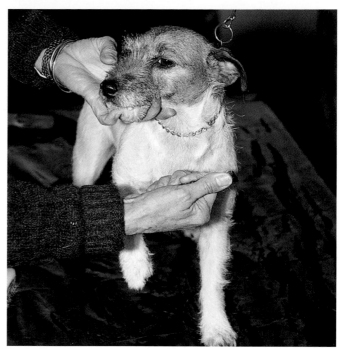
In plucking, the hair is grasped between the thumb and forefinger.

into the blood, or given orally, so that the flea dies when it sucks the blood. They, too, can produce toxicity and even kill the dog if used improperly. It is extremely important that you be aware of which chemicals in your arsenal are cholinesterase inhibitors. Using a yard spray in conjunction with systemics, or some sprays and dips, or with certain worm medications that are also cholinesterase inhibitors, can be a deadly combination. A new "spot-on" type flea control, marketed under the name "Advantage," is not absorbed into the dog but self-distributes throughout the coat. The manufacturer claims that the product is safe and water-resistant; initial reports are very encouraging.

Insect growth regulators (IGRs) prevent immature fleas from maturing and have proven to be the most highly

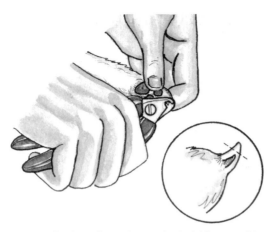

Cut the nails as close to the "quick" as possible.

effective method for long-term flea control. Precor is the most widely used for indoor applications, but is quickly broken down by ultraviolet light. Fenoxicarb is better for outdoor use because it is resistant to ultraviolet light. IGRs are nontoxic to mammals but tend to be expensive. A different

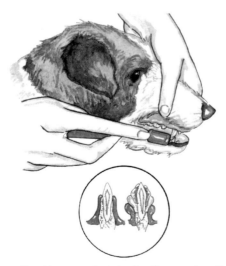

Brushing your dog's teeth will prevent costly dental procedures and disease. Left unattended, teeth can become seriously infected.

type of IGR are nematodes that eat flea larva. Studies show them to be effective and safe, but they must be reapplied regularly since they die when their food supply (the current crop of flea larva) is gone. Newest on the market is lufenuron, an IGR given to the dog orally once a month. Fleas feeding on the dog are sterilized, and lufenuron is extremely safe. It may takes months before seeing a change in the flea population, however, and all animals in the environment must be taking lufenuron.

One final warning: There is a popular product on the market that contains "deet" (diethyl-m-toluamide: the same chemical found in some human insect repellents). It has been implicated in the death of many dogs, and is not recommended for any dog.

Because only about 1 to 10 percent of your home's flea population is actually on your dog, you must concentrate on treating your home and yard. These are best treated with a combination adult flea killer and IGR. Cut grass short. Wash all pet bedding and vacuum other surfaces regularly, and especially before applying insecticides. Be sure that sprays reach into small crevices.

Tough as Nails

JRT nails were developed to withstand digging through and running over rocky terrain and hard-packed earth. Without this constant abrasion, they will grow overly long, causing discomfort, lameness, splayed feet, and painful split nails, and the toes will be more susceptible to injury. When you can hear the pitter-patter of clicking nails, that means that with every step the nails are hitting the floor, and you need to give nature a hand and cut those bear claws. If dewclaws are left untrimmed, they can get caught on things more easily or actually loop around and grow into the dog's leg. You must prevent this by trimming your dog's nails every week or two.

Start young. Begin by handling the feet and nails daily, and then cutting the very tips of your puppy's nails every week, taking special care not to cut the "quick" (the central core of blood vessels and nerve endings). You may find it easiest to cut the nails with your puppy lying on its back in your lap. With an adult, it is usually easier to hold the foot behind the dog, much like a blacksmith holds a horse's hoof. If you look at the bottoms of the nails you will see a solid core culminating in a hollowed nail. Cut the tip up to the core, but not beyond. On occasion you will slip up and cause the nail to bleed. This is best stopped by styptic powder or "shaving stick," but if this is not available dip the nail in flour, hold it to a wet tea bag, or drag it deep into a bar of soap.

Jack Plaque Attack

The accumulation of plaque and tartar is a major health problem in today's dogs. Dry food and hard dog biscuits, rawhide, and nylabone chewies are helpful, but not totally effective, at removing plaque. Brushing your JRT's teeth once or twice weekly (optimally, daily) with a child's toothbrush and special doggy toothpaste (available in pet stores or from your veterinarian) is the best plaque remover. If not removed, plaque will attract bacteria and minerals, which will harden into tartar. If you cannot brush, your veterinarian can supply cleansing solution that will help to kill plaque-forming bacteria, as well as bad breath! You may have to have your veterinarian clean your dog's teeth as often as once a year, especially often in older dogs.

Neglected plaque and tartar can cause infections to form along the gum line. The infection can gradually work its way down the sides of the tooth until the entire root is undermined. The tissues and bone around the tooth erode, and the tooth finally falls out. Meanwhile, the bacteria may have

entered the bloodstream and traveled throughout the body, causing infection in the kidneys and heart valves. Neglecting your dog's teeth can do more harm than simply causing bad breath; it could possibly kill your dog.

Between four and seven months of age, puppies will begin to shed their baby teeth and show off new permanent teeth. Often deciduous (baby) teeth, especially the canines (fangs), are not shed, so that the permanent tooth grows in beside the baby tooth. If this condition persists for over a week, consult your veterinarian. Retained baby teeth can cause misalignment of adult teeth.

Be Ear Responsible

The dog's ear canal is made up of an initial long vertical segment that then abruptly angles to run horizontally toward the skull. This configuration provides a moist environment in which various ear infections can flourish. The semi-prick ear of the JRT allows adequate air circulation, thwarting many infections, but even JRTs can develop painful and serious ear problems.

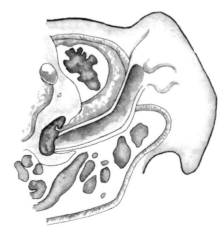

The dog's ear canal consists of an initial vertical canal, with an abrupt curve leading to a horizontal canal.

The road to a long life begins with good care in puppyhood.

Signs of Ear Problems

These include inflammation, discharge, debris, foul odor, pain, scratching, shaking, tilting of the head, or circling to one side. Extreme pain may indicate a ruptured ear drum. Bacterial and fungal infections, ear mites or ticks, foreign bodies, inhalant allergies, seborrhea, or hypothyroidism are possible underlying problems. Grass awns are one of the most common causes of ear problems in dogs that spend time outdoors. Keep the ear lubricated with mineral oil, and seek veterinary treatment as soon as possible. Ear problems only get worse.

Warning: Don't use cotton swabs in the ear canal, as they can irritate the skin and pack debris into the horizontal canal. Never use powders in the ear, which can cake, or hydrogen peroxide, which leaves the ear moist.

Ear Mites

Highly contagious and intensely irritating, ear mites are often found in puppies. Affected dogs will shake their head, scratch their ears, and carry their head sideways. A dark, dry, waxy buildup resembling coffee grounds in the ear canal, usually of both ears is the ear mite's signature. This material is actually dried blood mixed with ear wax. If you place some of this wax on a piece of dark paper, you may be able to see the tiny white moving culprits. Over-the-counter ear mite preparations can cause worse irritation. Ear mites are best treated by your veterinarian.

If you must treat the dog yourself, get a pyrethrin/mineral oil ear product. First flush the ear with an ear cleaning solution. You can buy a solution from your veterinarian, or make a mixture of one part alcohol to two parts white vinegar. Cleaning solutions will flush debris but will not kill mites or cure infections. Apply the ear mite drops daily for at least a week, and possibly a month. Because these mites are also found in the dog's fur all over its body, you should also bathe the pet weekly with a pyrethrin based shampoo, or apply a pyrethrin flea dip, powder, or spray. Separate a dog with ear mites from other pets and wash your hands after handling its ears. Ideally, every pet in a household should be treated.

The Smelly Dog

Doggy odor is not only offensive; it is unnatural. Don't exile the dog, or hold your breath. If a bath doesn't produce results, it's time to use your nose to pinpoint the source of the problem. Infection is a common cause of bad odor; check the mouth, ears, feet, and genitals. Generalized bad odor can indicate a skin problem, such as seborrhea. Don't ignore bad odor, and don't make your dog take the blame for something you need to fix. Of course, sometimes it's simply the result of the dog's well-known penchant for rolling in the most foul-smelling substances available, in which case a bath is the cure!

JRT maintenance requires a little attention often, rather than a lot of attention seldom. A few minutes a day can help you stop a problem before it develops.

Jack Russell Terrier Repair

Your dog can tell you where it hurts if you only know how to listen to it. You listen by means of a weekly health check and a regular veterinary checkup.

The Health Check

A weekly health check should be part of your grooming procedure. The health check should include examining:
- the eyes for discharge, cloudiness, or discolored "whites"
- the ears for bad smell, redness, or discharge
- the mouth for red, bleeding, or swollen gums, loose teeth, ulcers of the tongue or gums, or bad breath
- the nose for thickened or colored discharge
- the skin for parasites, hair loss, crusts, red spots, or lumps
- the feet for cuts, abrasions, split nails, bumps, or misaligned toes

Observe your dog for signs of lameness or incoordination, a sore neck, circling, loss of muscling, and for any behavioral change. Run your hands over the muscles and bones and check that they are symmetrical from one side to the other. Weigh your dog and observe whether it is putting on fat or wasting away. Check for any growths or swellings, which could be a sign of cancer or a number of less serious problems. A sore that does not heal, or any pigmented lump that begins to grow or bleed should be checked by a veterinarian immediately. Look out for mammary masses, changes in testicle size, discharge from the vulva or penis, increased or decreased urination, foul-smelling or strangely colored urine, incontinence, swollen abdomen, black or bloody stool, change in appetite or water consumption, difficulty breathing, lethargy, gagging, or loss of balance.

To take your dog's temperature, lubricate a rectal thermometer (preferably the digital type) and insert it about 1½ inches (3.8 cm), and leave it for about one minute. Do not allow your dog to sit down on the thermometer! Normal temperature for a JRT is around 101°F (38.3°C), ranging from 100 to 102.5°F (37.8°–39.2°C).

Always on its toes, the Jack Russell terrier never puts off till tomorrow what it can do today. When it comes to veterinary care, you should follow its example.

Move an injured dog carefully, preferably on a hard board. Use a blanket or towel if a board is not available. You can pull the dog onto it by the loose skin on its neck and back.

A good place to check the pulse is on the femoral artery, located inside the rear leg, where the thigh meets the abdomen. Normal pulse rates range from 80 to 100 beats per minute in an awake JRT, and are strong and fairly regular.

The Health Team

Your health check can go only so far in ensuring your pet's healthy status. A good veterinarian will also be needed to monitor your dog's internal signs by way of blood tests and other procedures.

When choosing your veterinarian, consider availability, emergency arrangements, costs, facilities, and ability to communicate. Some veterinarians will include more sophisticated tests as part of their regular checkups, but such tests, while desirable, will add to the cost of a visit. Unless money is no object, reach an understanding about procedures and fees before having them performed. You and your veterinarian will form a team who will work together to protect your JRT's health, so your rapport with your veterinarian is very important. Your veterinarian should listen to your observations, and should explain to you exactly what is happening with your dog. The clinic should be clean, and have safe, sanitary overnight accommodations. After-hour emergency arrangements should be made clear.

When you take your JRT to the veterinary clinic, hold your dog on your lap or in a cage; don't let it bark, mingle with, or frighten other animals, who may be sick. If you think your dog may have a contagious illness, inform the clinic beforehand so that you can use another entrance. Your veterinarian will be appreciative if your JRT is clean, parasite-free, and under control during the examination. Warn your veterinarian if you think there is any chance that your dog may bite.

Emergencies

In general:
• Know the phone number and location of the emergency veterinarian in your area. In fact, write it on the top of this page or put it on your refrigerator.
• Always keep enough fuel in your car to make it to the emergency clinic without having to stop to find a gas station.
• Make sure breathing passages are open. Remove any collar and check the mouth and throat.
• Be calm and reassuring. A calm dog is less likely to go into shock.
• Move the dog as little and as gently as possible.
• Control any bleeding.
• Check breathing, pulse, and consciousness.

• Check for signs of shock (very pale gums, weakness, unresponsiveness, faint pulse, shivering). Treat by keeping the dog warm and calm.
• Never use force or do anything that causes extreme discomfort.
• Never remove an impaled object (unless it is blocking the airway).

Severe Allergic Reaction

Insect stings are the most common cause of extreme reactions. Swelling around the nose and throat can block the airway. Other signs are restlessness, vomiting, diarrhea, seizures, and collapse. These symptoms indicate an emergency; call the veterinarian immediately.

Inability to Urinate

Blockage of urine can result in death. Inability to urinate is an emergency; call the veterinarian immediately.

Poisoning

Symptoms and treatment vary depending upon the specific poison. If possible, bring the poison and its container with you. If in doubt about whether poison was ingested, call the veterinarian anyway. The most common and life-threatening poison eaten by dogs is ethylene glycol (antifreeze). Veterinary treatment must be obtained within two to four hours of ingestion of even tiny amounts if the dog's life is to be saved.

Rodent and insect baits also attract dogs and require immediate veterinary attention.

Signs: Vary according to poison, but commonly include vomiting, convulsions, staggering, collapse

Treatment: Call the veterinarian or poison control hotline and give as much information as possible. You may need to induce vomiting (except in the cases outlined below) by giving either hydrogen peroxide (mixed 1:1 with water), salt water, or dry mustard and water. Treat for shock and get to the veterinarian at once. Be prepared for convulsions or respiratory distress.

Do not induce vomiting if the poison was an acid, alkali, petroleum product, solvent, cleaner, tranquilizer, or if a sharp object was swallowed; also do not induce vomiting if the dog is severely depressed, convulsing, comatose, or if over two hours have passed since ingestion. If the dog is not convulsing or unconscious dilute the poison by giving milk, vegetable oil, or egg whites. Activated charcoal can adsorb many toxins. Baking soda or milk of magnesia can be given for ingested acids, and vinegar or lemon juice for ingested alkalis.

The First Aid/Medical Kit

You should maintain a first aid/medical kit for your Jack Russell, which should contain:
• rectal thermometer
• scissors
• tweezer
• sterile gauze dressings
• self-adhesive bandage
• instant cold compress
• antidiarrhea medication (Immodium or prescription medication from your veterinarian)
• ophthalmic ointment (from your veterinarian)
• soap
• antiseptic skin ointment (from your veterinarian)
• hydrogen peroxide
• clean sponge
• pen light
• syringe
• towel
• stethoscope (optional)
• oxygen (optional)
• first aid instructions
• veterinarian and emergency clinic numbers
• poison control center number

HOW-TO:
Administering First Aid

For the following emergencies there may be no time to seek veterinary guidance. *Initiate first aid; then transport to the veterinarian immediately (call first).*

Breathing Difficulties
Signs: Gasping for breath with head extended, anxiety, weakness; advances to loss of consciousness, bluish tongue (Exception: Carbon monoxide poisoning causes bright red tongue).

Treatment: If not breathing, give mouth-to-nose resuscitation:

1. Open the dog's mouth, clear passage of secretions and foreign bodies.

2. Pull the tongue forward.

3. Seal your mouth over the dog's nose and mouth, blow gently into the dog's nose for three seconds, then release.

Cool a dog with heat stroke by covering it with wet towels and placing it in front of a fan. Dunking the dog in ice water is dangerous because it constricts peripheral blood vessels.

72

4. Continue until the dog breathes on its own.

If due to **drowning,** turn the dog upside down, holding it by the hind legs, so that water can run out of its mouth. Then administer mouth-to-nose resuscitation, with the dog's head positioned lower than its lungs.

For **obstructions,** wrap your hands around the abdomen, behind the rib cage, and compress briskly. Repeat if needed. If the dog loses consciousness, extend the head and neck forward, pull the tongue out fully, and explore the throat for any foreign objects.

Shock
Signs: Very pale gums, weakness, unresponsiveness, faint pulse, shivering.

Treatment: Keep the dog warm and calm; control any bleeding; check breathing, pulse, and consciousness and treat these problems if needed.

Gastric Dilatation/Torsion (Bloat)
Signs: Distended abdomen, restlessness, panting, salivation, attempts to vomit.

Treatment: Get the dog to the veterinarian immediately. Survival is directly related to promptness of treatment. The twisted stomach cuts off the blood supply to tissues, resulting in tissue death that may ultimately cause the dog's death. Passing a tube into the stomach to release gas may help as a preliminary measure in some cases.

Heat Stroke
Signs: Rapid, loud breathing; abundant thick saliva, bright red mucous membranes, high rectal temperature. **Later signs:** Unsteadiness, diarrhea, coma.

Treatment: Cover the dog with a cold wet towel and place it in front of a fan. If this is not possible, immerse the dog in cool water. *Do not plunge the dog in ice water.* Offer small amounts of water for drinking. You must lower your dog's body temperature quickly (but do not lower it below 100°F [37.8·C]).

Hypothermia
Signs: Shivering, cold feeling, sluggishness.

Treatment: Warm gradually. Wrap the dog in a blanket. Place plastic bottles filled with hot water outside the blankets (not touching the dog). You can also place a plastic wrap over the blanket, making sure the dog's head is not covered. Don't use heat lamps, which too often result in burns or excessive heating. Monitor temperature with thermometer.

Convulsions or Seizures
Signs: Drooling, stiffness, muscle spasms.

Treatment: Wrap the dog securely in a blanket to prevent it from injuring itself on furniture or stairs. Remove other dogs from the area (they may attack the convulsing dog). Never put your hands (or anything) in a convulsing dog's mouth. Monitor for shock. Make note of all characteristics and sequences of seizure activity, which can help to diagnose the cause.

Eye Injuries
For contact with irritants, flush for five minutes with water or saline solution. For injuries,

cover with clean gauze soaked in water or saline solution.

Hypoglycemia (Low Blood Sugar)

Signs: The dog appears disoriented, weak, staggering. It may appear blind, and the muscles may twitch. Later stages lead to convulsions, coma, and death. Most often seen in small dogs, or dogs that have been very active and have not been fed.

Treatment: Give food, or honey or syrup mixed with warm water.

Open Wounds

Signs: Consider wounds to be an emergency if there is profuse bleeding, if extremely deep, if open to chest cavity, abdominal cavity, or head.

Treatment: Control massive bleeding first. Cover the wound with clean dressing and apply pressure; apply more dressings over the others until bleeding stops. Also elevate the wound site, and apply cold pack to site. If an extremity, apply pressure to the closest pressure point as follows:

• for a front leg—inside of front leg just above the elbow
• for a rear leg—inside of thigh where the femoral artery crosses the thigh bone
• for the tail—underside of tail close to where it joins the body

Use a tourniquet only in life-threatening situations and when all other attempts have failed. Check for signs of shock.

Sucking chest wounds: Place sheet of plastic or other nonporous material over the hole and bandage it to make as air-tight a seal as possible.

Apply pressure to the closest pressure point for uncontrolled bleeding of an extremity.

Abdominal wounds: Place warm, wet, sterile dressing over any protruding internal organs; cover with bandage or towel. Do not attempt to push organs back into the dog.

Head wounds: Apply gentle pressure to control bleeding. Monitor for loss of consciousness or shock and treat accordingly.

Electrical Shock

Signs: Collapse, burns inside mouth.

Treatment: Before touching the dog, disconnect plug or cut power; if that cannot be done immediately, use a wooden pencil, spoon, or broom handle to knock cord away from dog. Keep the dog warm and treat for shock. Monitor breathing and heartbeat.

Poisonous Snakebites

Signs: Swelling, discoloration, pain, fangmarks, restlessness, nausea, weakness.

Treatment: Restrain the dog and keep it quiet. Be able to describe the snake. Only if you can't get to the veterinarian, apply a pressure bandage between the bite and the heart, tight enough to prevent blood from returning to the heart. For dogs bitten on the muzzle, a pressure bandage is not feasable. Never use a tourniquet.

Deep Burns

Signs: Charred or pearly white skin; deeper layers of tissue exposed.

Treatment: Cool the burned area with cool packs, towels soaked in ice water, or by immersing in cold water. If over 50 percent of the dog is burned, do not immerse as this may cause shock. Cover the area with clean bandage or towel to avoid contamination. Do not apply pressure; do not apply ointments. Monitor for shock.

Other Potential Emergencies

In the following situations, *administer first aid*, then call your veterinarian to see if your dog should be seen on an emergency basis. This will depend upon the severity and extensiveness of the problem.

Animal bites: Allow some bleeding. Clean the area thoroughly. Antibiotic therapy will probably be necessary.

Insect stings: Remove any visible stingers. Administer baking soda and water paste to bee stings, and vinegar to wasp stings. Clean area and apply antibacterial ointment. Monitor for allergic reaction.

Situations not described in this list can usually be treated with the same first aid as for humans. *In all cases, the best advice is to seek the opinion of a veterinarian.*

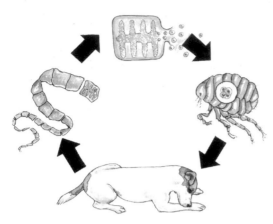

The life-cycle of the tapeworm. Note that a flea is a necessary intermediate host.

Preventive Medicine

The best preventive medicine is that which prevents accidents: a well-trained dog in a securely fenced yard or on a leash, and a properly terrier-proofed home. However, other preventive steps must be taken to avoid diseases and parasites.

Medications

When giving pills, open your dog's mouth and place the pill well to the back and in the middle of the tongue. Close the mouth and gently stroke the throat until your dog swallows. Pre-wetting capsules or better, covering them with cream cheese or some similar food, helps prevent capsules from sticking to the tongue or roof of the mouth. For liquid medicine, tilt the head back and place the liquid in the pouch of the cheek. Then close your dog's mouth until it swallows. Always give the full course of medications prescribed by your veterinarian. Don't give your dog human medications unless you have been directed to do so by your veterinarian as some medications for humans have no effect upon dogs, and some can have a very detrimental effect.

Vaccinations

Rabies, distemper, leptospirosis, canine hepatitis, parvovirus, and corona virus are highly contagious and deadly diseases that have broken many a loving owner's heart in the past. Now that vaccinations are available for these maladies, one would think they would no longer be a threat, but many dogs remain unvaccinated and continue to succumb to and spread these potentially fatal illnesses. Don't let your Jack Russell Terrier be one of them.

Vaccinations are also available for kennel cough and Lyme disease, but may be optional depending upon your dog's lifestyle. Your veterinarian can advise you. Always make sure your dog is in good health at the time it is vaccinated. Many dogs seem to feel under the weather for a day or so after receiving their vaccinations, so don't schedule your appointment the day before boarding, a trip, or a big doggy event.

Puppies receive their dam's immunity through nursing in the first days of life. This is why it is important that your pup's mother be properly immunized before breeding, and that your pup be able to nurse from its dam. The immunity gained from the mother will wear off after several weeks, and then the pup will be susceptible to disease unless you provide immunity through vaccinations. The problem is that there is no way to know exactly when this passive immunity will wear off, and vaccinations given before that time are ineffective. So you must revaccinate over a period of weeks so that your pup will not be unprotected and will receive lasting immunity.

Your pup's breeder will have given the first vaccinations to your pup before it was old enough to go home with you. Bring all information about your pup's vaccination history to your veterinarian on your first visit so that the pup's vaccination schedule can be maintained.

Meanwhile, it is best not to let your pup mingle with strange dogs.

Internal Parasite Control

Heartworms: Heartworms are a deadly nematode parasite carried by mosquitoes; therefore, wherever mosquitoes are present, dogs should be on heartworm prevention. Several effective types of heartworm preventive are available, with some also preventing many other types of worms. Ask your veterinarian when your puppy should begin taking the preventive. If you forget to give it as prescribed, your dog may get heartworms. A dog with suspected heartworms should not be given the preventive because a fatal reaction could occur. Heartworms are treatable in their early stages, but the treatment is expensive and not without risks (although a less risky treatment has recently become available). If untreated, heartworms can kill your pet.

Intestinal parasites: Hookworms, whipworms, ascarids, threadworms, and lungworms are all types of nematode parasites that can infect dogs of all ages, but have their most devastating effect on puppies. When you take the pup to be vaccinated, bring along a stool specimen so that your veterinarian can also check for these parasites. Most puppies do have worms at some point, even pups from the most fastidious breeders. This is because some types of larval worms become encysted in the dam's body long before she ever became pregnant, perhaps when she herself was a pup. Here they lie dormant and immune from worming, until hormonal changes due to her pregnancy cause them to be activated, and then they infect her fetuses or her newborns through her milk. You may be tempted to pick up some worm medication and worm your puppy yourself. Don't. Over-the-counter wormers are largely ineffective and

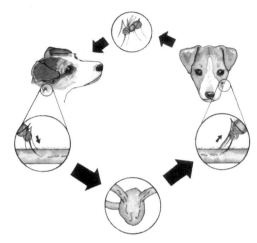

The life cycle of heartworms. When a mosquito bites an infected dog, it ingests circulating immature heartworms, which it then passs on to the next dog it bites.

often more dangerous than those available through your veterinarian. Left untreated, worms can cause vomiting, diarrhea, dull coat, listlessness, anemia, and death. Have your puppy tested for internal parasites regularly. Some heartworm preventives also prevent most types of intestinal worms (but not tapeworms).

Tapeworms (cestodes) tend to plague some dogs throughout their lives. There is no preventive, except to diligently rid your JRT of fleas, because fleas transmit tapeworms to dogs. Some tapeworms can also be contracted from rodent, deer, and rabbit carcasses. Tapeworms look like moving white worms on fresh stools, or may dry up and look like rice grains around the dog's anus. Tapeworms are one of the least harmful worms, but their segments can be irritating to the dog's anal region, and are certainly unsightly.

Common Misconceptions about Worms

• **Misconception:** A dog that is "scooting" its rear along the ground

The grass is always greener. Make sure poisonous plants aren't on the other side of the fence.

has worms. Although this may be a sign of tapeworms, a dog that repeatedly scoots more likely has impacted anal sacs.

• **Misconception:** Feeding a dog sugar and sweets will give it worms. There are good reasons not to feed a dog sweets, but worms have nothing to do with them.

• **Misconception:** Dogs should be regularly wormed every month or so.

Dogs should be wormed when, and only when, they have been diagnosed with worms. No worm medication is completely without risk, and it is foolish to use it carelessly.

Protozoa: Puppies and dogs also suffer from protozoan parasites, such as coccidia and especially, *Giardia*. These can cause chronic or intermittent diarrhea, and can be diagnosed with a stool specimen.

Sample Vaccination Schedule

Age (weeks)	Vaccine
6–8	distemper + hepatitis + parainfluenza + parvovirus
10–12	distemper + hepatitis + parainfluenza + parvovirus + leptospirosis
14–16	distemper + hepatitis + parainfluenza + parvovirus + leptospirosis, rabies
18–20	distemper + hepatitis + parainfluenza + parvovirus + leptospirosis

Note: Boosters must be given annually.

Common Ailments and Symptoms

Coughing

Allergies, foreign bodies, pneumonia, tracheal collapse, tumors, and especially, kennel cough and heart disease, can all cause coughing.

Kennel cough is a highly communicable airborne disease caused by several different infectious agents, but all cause similar symptoms. It is characterized by a gagging cough arising eight days after exposure. Inoculations are available and are an especially good idea if you plan to have your dog around other dogs at training classes or while being boarded.

Heart disease can result in coughing, most often in older dogs following exercise or in the evening. The dog will often lie down with its head pointed upward. Treatment with diuretics prescribed by your veterinarian can help alleviate the coughing for a while.

Any persistent cough should be checked by your veterinarian. Coughing irritates the throat and can lead to secondary infections if allowed to continue unchecked. It can also be miserable for the dog.

Vomiting

Vomiting is a common occurrence that may or may not indicate a serious problem. Vomiting after eating grass is common and usually of no great concern. Overeating is a common cause of occasional vomiting in puppies, especially if they follow eating with playing. Feed smaller meals more frequently if this becomes a problem. Vomiting immediately after meals could indicate an obstruction of the esophagus. Repeated vomiting could indicate that the dog has eaten spoiled food, undigestible objects, or may have a stomach illness. Veterinary advice should be sought. Meanwhile, withhold food (or feed as directed for diarrhea) and restrict water.

Consult your veterinarian immediately if your dog vomits a foul substance resembling fecal matter (indicating a blockage in the intestinal tract), blood (partially digested blood resembles coffee grounds), or if there is projectile or continued vomiting. Sporadic vomiting with poor appetite and generally poor condition could indicate internal parasites or a more serious internal disease that should also be checked by your veterinarian.

Diarrhea

Diarrhea can result from overexcitement or nervousness, a change in diet or water, sensitivity to certain foods, overeating, intestinal parasites, viral or bacterial infections, or ingestion of

Just horsin' around. Dogs and horses should be introduced carefully. A kick can spell death for a small dog.

toxic substances. Bloody diarrhea, diarrhea with vomiting, fever, or other signs of toxicity, or diarrhea that lasts for more than a day should not be allowed to continue without veterinary advice. Some of these could be symptomatic of potentially fatal disorders.

Less severe diarrhea can be treated at home by withholding or severely restricting food and water for 24 hours. Ice cubes can be given to satisfy thirst. Administer Immodium in the same weight dosage as recommended for humans. A bland diet consisting of rice, tapioca, or cooked macaroni, along with cottage cheese or tofu for protein, should be given for several days. Feed nothing else. The intestinal tract needs time off in order to heal.

Urinary Tract Diseases

If your dog has difficulty or pain in urination, urinates suddenly and often but in small amounts, or passes cloudy or bloody urine, it may be suffering from a problem of the bladder, urethra, or prostate. Dribbling of urine during sleep indicates a hormonal problem. Urinalysis and a rectal exam by your veterinarian are necessary to diagnose the exact nature of the problem. Bladder infections must be treated promptly to prevent the infection from reaching the kidneys.

Kidney disease, ultimately leading to kidney failure, is one of the most common ailments of older dogs. The earliest symptom is usually increased urination. Although the excessive urination may cause problems in keeping your house clean or your night's sleep intact, *never* try to restrict water from a dog with kidney disease. Increased urination can also be a sign of diabetes or a urinary tract infection. Your veterinarian can discover the cause with some simple tests, and each of these conditions can be treated. For kidney disease, a low-protein and low-sodium diet can slow the progression.

In males, infections of the *prostate gland* can lead to repeated urinary tract infections, and sometimes painful defecation or blood and pus in the urine. Castration and long-term antibiotic therapy is required for improvement.

Impacted Anal Sacs

Constant licking of the anus or scooting along the ground are characteristic signs of anal sac impaction. Dogs have two anal sacs that are normally emptied by rectal pressure during defecation. Their musky smelling contents may also be forcibly ejected when a dog is extremely frightened. Sometimes they fail to empty properly and become impacted or infected. This is more common in small dogs, obese dogs, dogs with seborrhea, and dogs that seldom have firm stools. Impacted sacs cause extreme discomfort and can become infected. Treatment consists of manually emptying the sacs and administering antibiotics. As a last resort, the sacs may be removed surgically.

Endocrine Disorders

The most widespread hormone related disorders in dogs are diabetes, hypothyroidism, and Cushing's syndrome.

Hypothyroidism, the most common of these, also has the least obvious symptoms, which may include weight gain, lethargy, and coat problems such as oiliness, dullness, *symmetrical* hair loss, and hair that is easily pulled out.

The hallmark of diabetes is increased drinking and urination, and sometimes increased appetite with weight loss. It is most common in obese spayed females.

Cushing's syndrome (hyperadrenocorticism) is seen mostly in older dogs, and is characterized by increased drinking and urination, a potbellied appearance, symmetrical hair loss on the body, darkened skin, and susceptibility to infections.

All of these conditions can be diagnosed with simple tests, and can be treated by your veterinarian with drugs.

Eye Problems

A watery discharge can be a symptom of a foreign body, allergies, corneal ulcer, or a tear drainage problem. If accompanied by squinting or pawing at the eye, suspect a foreign body in it. Examine under the lids and flood the eye with saline solution, or use a moist cotton swab to remove any debris. A clogged tear drainage duct can cause the tears to drain onto the face, rather than the normal drainage through the nose. Your veterinarian can diagnose a drainage problem with a simple test.

KCS: A thick ropey mucous or crusty discharge suggests conjunctivitis or dry eye (*keratoconjunctivitis sicca,* or KCS). In KCS there is inadequate tear production, resulting in irritation to the surface of the eye whenever the dog blinks. The surface of the eye may appear dull. KCS can cause secondary bacterial infection or corneal ulcers. In fact, KCS should be suspected in any dog in which recurrent corneal ulceration or conjunctivitis is a problem. In past years, treatment of KCS was with the frequent application of artificial tears, which most owners found difficult to perform as often as needed. Recent drug advances treat KCS with ophthalmic immunosuppressive therapy. This therapy can be quite effective if begun early.

Cataracts: As your JRT ages it is natural that the lens of the eye becomes a little hazy. You will notice this as a slightly grayish appearance behind the pupils. But if this occurs at a young age, or if the lens looks white or opaque, ask your veterinarian to check your dog for cataracts. In cataracts the lens becomes so opaque that light can no longer reach the retina. As in humans, the lens can be surgically removed. It can also be replaced with an artificial lens, but most dogs seem to do well without replacement.

Lens luxation is an inherited disorder in Jack Russells and many other terriers. The lens is normally held in place behind the iris by a ring of thin fibers (called zonules), but if these attachments are lost the lens will float out of position, sometimes even protruding through the pupil. A totally displaced ("luxated") lens is painful; the eye will be red and possibly opaque. If vision is to be saved, the lens must be removed immediately. A partially displaced ("subluxated") lens has less obvious symptoms, and may be treated medically. Dogs with either condition, unless obviously arising from trauma, should not be bred.

Any time your dog's pupils do not constrict in response to light, or when one eye reacts differently from another, take it to the veterinarian immediately. It could indicate a serious ocular or neurological problem.

Limping

Limping may or may not indicate a serious problem. Mild lameness should be treated by complete rest; if it still persists after three days, your dog will need to be examined by the veterinarian. When associated with extreme pain, fever, swelling, deformity, or grinding or popping sounds, you should have your veterinarian examine your JRT at once. Ice packs may help minimize swelling if applied immediately after an injury.

Fractures should be immobilized by splinting above and below the site of fracture (small rolled magazines work well on legs) before moving the dog. Immediate veterinary attention is required.

Knee injuries are common in dogs; most do not get well on their own.

Avoid pain medications that might encourage the use of an injured limb.

Puppies are especially susceptible to bone and joint injuries, and should never be allowed to jump from high places or run until exhausted. Persistent limping in puppies may result from one of several developmental bone problems, and should be checked by the veterinarian. Both puppies and adults should be kept from playing and running on slippery floors that could cause them to lose their footing.

Osteoarthritis: In older dogs, or dogs with a previous injury, limping is often the result of osteoarthritis. Arthritis can be treated with aspirin, but should be done so only under veterinary supervision. Do not use naxopren. Any time a young or middle aged dog shows signs of arthritis, especially in a joint that has not been previously injured, it should be examined by its veterinarian.

Also see discussion of skin, ear, and dental problems, pages 63–64, 67–68, and 67.

The Old Friend

The spry JRT ages well and lives long. Eventually, though, you will notice that your dog sleeps longer and more soundly than it did as a youngster. Upon awakening, it is slower to get going and may be stiff at first. It may be less eager to play and more content to lie in the sun. It may even become obedient!

Both physical activity and metabolic rates decrease in older animals, meaning that they require fewer calories to maintain the same weight. It is important to keep your older dog active. Older dogs that are fed the same as when they were young risk becoming obese; they have a greater risk of cardiovascular and joint problems, and metabolic diseases.

Older dogs should be fed several small meals instead of one large meal, and should be fed on time. Moistening dry food or feeding canned food can help a dog with dental problems enjoy its meal.

Although many geriatric dogs are overweight, others lose weight and may need to eat a special diet in order to keep the pounds on. Most older dogs do not require a special diet unless they have a particular medical need for it (such as obesity: low calorie; kidney failure: low protein; heart failure: low sodium).

Arthritis: Arthritis is a common cause of intermittent stiffness and lameness. A soft warm bed combined with moderate activity can help, and your veterinarian can prescribe drugs for severe cases.

Odors: Older dogs tend to have a stronger body odor, but you should not just ignore increased odors. They could indicate specific problems, such as periodontal disease, impacted anal sacs, seborrhea, ear infections, or even kidney disease. Any strong odor should be checked by your veterinarian. Like people, dogs lose skin moisture as they age, and though dogs don't have to worry about wrinkles, their skin can become dry and itchy. Regular brushing can help by stimulating oil production.

Immune system: The immune system may be less effective in older dogs, so it is increasingly important to shield your dog from infectious disease, chilling, overheating, and any stressful conditions.

Anesthesia risk: Older dogs present a somewhat greater anesthesia risk. Most of this increased risk can be negated, however, by first screening dogs with a complete medical workup.

Vomiting and diarrhea in an old dog can signal many different problems. Keep in mind that a small older dog cannot tolerate the dehydration that results from continued vomiting or diarrhea and you should not let it continue unchecked. The older dog should be seen by its veterinarian at least twice a year. Blood tests can detect early stages of diseases that can benefit from treatment.

Some older dogs become cranky and less patient, especially when dealing with puppies or boisterous children. But don't just excuse behavioral changes, especially if sudden, as due simply to aging. They could be symptoms of pain or disease.

Impaired senses: Older dogs may experience hearing or visual loss. Be careful not to startle a dog with impaired senses, as a startled dog could snap in self-defense. The slight haziness that appears in the older dog's pupils is normal and has minimal effect upon vision, but some dogs, especially those with diabetes, may develop cataracts. These can be removed by a veterinary ophthalmologist if they are severe. Decreased tear production increases the chances of KCS (dry eye) (see page 79). Dogs with gradual vision loss can cope well as long as they are kept in familiar surroundings, and extra safety precautions are followed.

Long trips may be grueling, and boarding in a kennel may be extremely upsetting. Introduction of a puppy or new pet may be welcomed and encourage your older dog to play, but if your dog is not used to other dogs the newcomer will more likely be resented and be an additional source of stress.

In general, any ailment that an older dog has is magnified in severity compared to the same symptoms in a younger dog. Don't be lulled into a false sense of security just because you own a Jack Russell terrier and they are usually known to live long lives. A long life depends upon good genes, good care, and good luck.

If you are lucky enough to have an old JRT, you still must accept that an end will come. Heart disease, kidney

Common Symptoms and Ailments of Older Dogs
- Diarrhea: kidney or liver disease, pancreatitis
- Coughing: heart disease, tracheal collapse, lung cancer
- Difficulty eating: periodontal disease, oral tumors
- Decreased appetite: kidney, liver, or heart disease, pancreatitis, cancer
- Increased appetite: diabetes, Cushing's syndrome
- Weight loss: heart, liver or kidney disease, diabetes, cancer
- Abdominal distension: heart or kidney disease, Cushing's syndrome, tumor
- Increased urination: diabetes, kidney or liver disease, cystitis, Cushing's syndrome
- Limping: arthritis, patellar luxation
- Nasal discharge: tumor, periodontal disease

failure, and cancer eventually claim most of these senior citizens. Early detection can help delay their effects, but unfortunately, can seldom prevent them ultimately.

Saying Farewell
Jack Russell terriers live a long time, but they do not live forever. Despite the best of care, a time will come when neither you nor your veterinarian can prevent your cherished pet from succumbing to old age or an incurable illness. It seems hard to believe that you will have to say good-bye to one who has been such a focal point of your life—in truth, a real member of your family. That dogs live such a short time compared to humans is a cruel fact, but one that all owners must ultimately face.

You should realize that both of you have been fortunate to have shared so many good times, but make sure that your JRT's remaining time is still plea-surable. Many terminal illnesses make your dog very ill indeed, and there comes a point where your desire to keep your friend with you as long as possible may not be the kindest thing for either of you. If your dog no longer eats its dinner or treats, it is a sign that it does not feel well and you must face the prospect of doing what is best for your beloved friend.

Euthanasia is a difficult and personal decision that no one wishes to make, and no one can make for you. Ask your veterinarian if there is a reasonable chance of your dog getting better, and if it is likely that your dog is suffering. Ask yourself if your dog is getting plea-sure out of life, and if it enjoys most of its days. Financial considerations can be a factor if it means going into debt in exchange for just a little while longer. Your own emotional state must also be considered.

If you do decide that euthanasia is the kindest farewell gift for your beloved friend, discuss with your vet-erinarian beforehand what will happen. Euthanasia is painless and involves giving an overdose of an anesthetic. If your dog is fearful of the veterinarian clinic, you might feel better having the doctor meet you at home or come out to your car. Although it won't be easy, try to remain with your dog so that its last moments will be filled with your love; otherwise, have a friend your Jack Russell knows stay with it. Try to recall the wonderful times you have shared and realize that, however painful losing such a once-in-a-lifetime

dog is, it is better than never having had such a partner at all.

Many people who regarded their JRT as a member of the family nonetheless feel embarrassed at the grief they feel at its loss. Yet this dog has often func-tioned as a surrogate child, best friend, and confidant. Partnership with a pet can be one of the closest and most stable relationships in many people's lives. Because people are often closer to their pets than they are to distant family members, it is not uncommon to feel more grief at the loss of the pet. Unfortunately, the support from friends that comes with human loss is too often absent with pet loss. Such well-meaning but ill-informed statements as "he was just a dog" or "just get another one" do little to ease the pain, but the truth is that many people simply don't know how to react and probably aren't really as callous as they might sound. There are, however, many people who share your feelings and there are pet bereavement counselors avail-able at many veterinary schools.

After losing such a cherished friend, many people say they will never get another dog. True, no dog will ever take the place of your dog. But you will find that another JRT is a welcome diversion and will help keep you from dwelling on the loss of your first pet, as long as you don't keep comparing the new dog to the old. True also, by getting another Jack Russell you are sentencing yourself to the same grief in another 10 to 15 years, but wouldn't you rather have that than miss out on a second once-in-a-lifetime dog?

The Next Generation

The Worst Idea You'll Ever Have

The compulsion so many people have to breed a litter is one of the most unfortunate aspects of dog ownership. Often, the decision to breed is done with little foresight or responsibility, and usually the result is a grave disservice to the breeders, their pet, the breed, the resulting puppies, and to their new owners. Unless you have studied dogs in general, and JRTs in particular, have proven your female to be a superior specimen in terms of conformation, health, and temperament, and plan to take responsibility for each and every puppy for the rest of its life, you have no business doing anything but having your dog neutered.

Why You Don't Want to Breed Your JRT

Before you proceed with plans to breed your JRT, consider the following:
• There are many more Jack Russell terriers born than there are good homes for them; therefore, the puppy you sell to a less than perfect buyer may end up neglected, abused, or discarded.
• The fact that your JRT is purebred and registered does not mean it is breeding quality, any more than the fact that you have a driver's license qualifies you to build race cars. Review the definition of breeding quality on page 14.
• JRTs typically have from five to seven puppies. Breeding so you can keep only one puppy ignores the

fact that six others may not get a good home.
• Selling a litter will probably not come close to reimbursing you for the stud fee, prenatal care, possible whelping complications, Caesarean sections, supplemental feeding, puppy food, vaccinations, advertising, and a staggering investment of time and energy.
• Responsible breeders have spent years researching genetics and the breed, breed only the best specimens, and screen for hereditary defects in order to obtain superior puppies. Until you have done the same, you are undoing the hard work of those who have dedicated their lives to bettering the breed.
• There is definite discomfort and some danger when whelping a litter. Watching a litter being born is *not* a good way to teach the children the miracle of life—there are too many things that can go wrong.
• A spayed female is much less likely to develop breast cancer and a number of other hormone-related diseases. She should be spayed before her first season in order to avoid these problems.

Breeding the Right Way

Ethical breeders breed a litter only after studying the breed standard, studying pedigrees, and studying individual dogs to find the most advantageous match of conformation, temperament, hunting ability, and health, then proving the worth of both prospective parents through competitions. They interview prospective buyers and get

A carefully planned litter is a source of pride, but seldom a source of income.

deposits from them before the breeding even takes place. They have money set aside for prenatal and postnatal care, and emergency funds and vacation time available for whelping or post-whelping complications. They have the commitment to keep every single puppy born for the rest of its life should good homes not be available or should they ever have to be returned. And they worry a lot. Is it any wonder that some of the best breeders breed the least?

Most people breed the wrong way. This is why so many purebred dogs are beset with problems, and animal shelters are flooded with unwanted dogs. These "backyard breeders" take a few dollars to the bank, pat themselves on the back, and take advantage of their "pet" by breeding her again her next season.

If you still have not been dissuaded from breeding your JRT, you owe it to yourself, your puppy buyers, and the breed to settle for no less than the best

available JRT stud. You will not find this stud advertised in the newspaper. If you are contemplating breeding it is assumed that you have now learned enough about the breed that you are familiar with prominent kennels and studs. Look for a stud that is superior in the areas your bitch needs improvement. Look for a stud owner who is honest about the stud's faults, health, and temperament. A responsible stud owner will have proven the stud by earning titles, will have complete records and photos of other litters the stud has produced, and will insist that your bitch and her pedigree be compatible before accepting her for breeding.

Both dogs to be bred should have a blood test for canine brucellosis, a primarily (but not exclusively) sexually transmitted disease with devastating effects on fertility. The female should also have a pre-breeding checkup to ensure that she is in good health, has current vaccinations, and does not

Will they live long and happy lives, weaving their ways into the hearts of their new families? Or will they be abused, discarded, and left to fate's whimsy? The choice is yours. Place them carefully, or don't bring them into the world.

have any abnormalities that would make for a difficult pregnancy. Long before your female comes into season you should have a written contract with the stud dog owner that spells out what fees will be due and when, and what will happen if no puppies are born.

Don't breed your female on her first season, or at least until she is two years of age, or if she is past seven years of age, and don't breed her on consecutive seasons. Even the best brood bitches are rarely bred more than three times in their life.

Remember that the JRTCA will not register inbred Jack Russells. They define this as dogs resulting from father/daughter, mother/son, or brother/sister matings. Half brother/half sister matings are permissible only once every three generations.

Dating, Mating, and Waiting
Signs of "heat" (estrus) begin with swelling of the vulva followed by a bloody discharge. Most females are breedable for several days sometime between the eighth and eighteenth day of estrus, although earlier and later alliances have been known to result in pregnancy. As she approaches her receptive stage, she will tend to "flag" her tail, or cock it to the side when the male approaches or if you scratch around the base of her tail. Your veterinarian can monitor her breeding stage with vaginal smears or blood tests. Your best indicator is the stud dog; experienced stud dogs do not need calendars or microscopes!

Breeding dogs involves more than just letting a male and female loose together. Although this may seem like the natural way, in fact it is not natural for two dogs to breed when they may have just met each other. Neither dog knows the other well enough to trust its actions, so the female will often snap in fear when the male mounts, and the male may be injured or dissuaded from

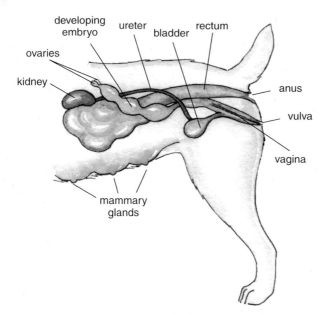

developing embryo ureter bladder rectum

ovaries

kidney

anus

vulva

vagina

mammary glands

Female reproductive organs. The ovary and uterus are removed in spaying.

mounting. Instead, after an initial period for introductions, the female should be held for the male, and muzzled if she appears to want to snap.

The Tie

After the male achieves intromission, he will step quickly back and forth from one leg to the other. Following this period of activity, he will want to dismount from the female. The dog's penis has a bulb near the base that swells with blood upon intromission, so that it is too large to fit back out through the muscles around the vaginal opening. Thus, the dogs remain "tied" until enough blood leaves the bulb for it to become small enough to slide out. This can take from 5 minutes to 45 minutes, but most commonly from 10 to 20 minutes. This is perfectly normal, and attempts to separate tied dogs can injure them and are usually futile. Keep both dogs comfortable and quiet during the tie, as the

male can be injured by the female's activity. After the dogs separate, make sure the male's penis goes back into its sheath and does not have hair turned in upon it.

For optimal chances of conception repeat the breeding every other day until the female will no longer accept the male. Be sure to keep her away from other males during this time— dogs are not known for their fidelity! Also, dogs from litters fathered by more than one sire cannot be registered.

The Waiting Game

Now you have two months to wait and plan. Gradually increase and change the expectant mother's food to a high-quality puppy food, or better, a food developed for pregnancy and lactation, as time progresses. Keep her in shape, as a well-conditioned dog will have fewer problems whelping. From 20 to 25 days post-breeding, your veterinarian may be able to feel the developing puppies, but this is not always accurate. Two encouraging signs of pregnancy that might appear at around 35 days post-breeding are a clear mucous discharge from the vagina and enlarged, pink nipples. If at any time the discharge is not clear, seek veterinary attention at once.

Avoid letting the mother-to-be jump down from high places after the first month. When carrying her be sure that you are not putting pressure on her abdomen. Do not give any medication without your veterinarian's advice. Your pregnant female should be isolated from strange dogs beginning three weeks before her due date; exposure to certain viruses during that time does not allow her to develop sufficient immunity to pass to her puppies, and can result in the loss of the litter.

Many females are prone to *false pregnancy,* a condition in which the breasts become slightly enlarged and may even have some milk. Pronounced cases involving large amounts of milk production, weight gain, and even nesting behavior and the adoption of certain toys as "babies" may be unhealthy and should be checked by your veterinarian. Some can be so convincing that even experienced breeders have thought their bitch was in whelp until she failed to deliver puppies!

Special Deliveries

Talk to your veterinarian or an experienced JRT breeder about what to expect at whelping. You should prepare a whelping box that will double as a nursery, and place it in a warm, quiet room. You can use the bottom of a plastic dog cage, a sturdy clean cardboard box, or a child's wading pool. The sides should be high enough so that the young pups cannot get out, but low enough so that the mother can get over without scraping her hanging nipples. The best whelping boxes include a "pig rail" around the sides so that the dam cannot accidentally lie on a puppy. Place the box on a rug or other insulating material, and line the inside with newspaper (blank is best, never colored), or preferably washable towels. Don't use indoor outdoor carpeting, which tends to interact with urine in such a way as to irritate pups' skin.

The whelping kit should include:
- highlighted whelping instructions
- emergency phone numbers
- rectal thermometer
- many towels and washcloths
- nasal aspirator
- scissors
- dental floss
- heating pad
- bitch's milk replacement

Average canine gestation time is 63 days from the first breeding, but there is some variability, with small dogs tending to be somewhat early rather than late. A more accurate prediction can be made from counting the days from the first day of diestrus, one of the phases of the estrus cycle. This

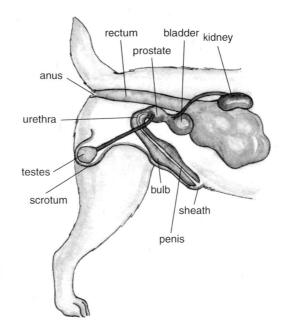

Male reproductive organs. The testicles are removed in castration.

day can be pinpointed by your veterinarian, but you must begin the procedure near the beginning of her season.

Labor

You can get about 12 hours advance notice by charting the expectant mother's temperature starting around the fifty-sixth day. Take her temperature three times a day, at the same times of day. When her temperature drops to about 98°F (36.7°C) and remains there, make plans to stay home because labor should begin within 12 hours. Warm the whelping box to 80°F (26.7°C), and prepare for a long night. She will become more restless, pant, nest, dig, pace, refuse to eat, and repeatedly demand to go out. Make her as comfortable as possible and do not let her go outside alone where she might have a puppy.

You can run, but you can't hide, from a Jack Russell terrier. This is the last thing seen by many small rodents.

The birth of puppies is messy, so at this point you should remove any blankets you wish to save. As labor becomes more intense, she may scratch and bite at her bedding. The puppies are preceded by a water bag. Once this has burst, the first puppy should be born soon. Your primary role is to be there for moral support and to make sure all goes well. The less you interfere, the better.

The Puppies Are Born

As each pup is born, watch that the mother clears its face so it can breathe. You can let the dam chew the cord, but if she neglects to do so, you can tie off the umbilical cord about ¾ inch (19 mm) from the puppy with dental floss, and then cut it on the side away from the pup. If you can't tie the cord, crush the cord with hemostats or sterilized pliers, then cut it with scissors, keeping the crushed area between the pup and the cut. The crushing action prevents the cord from bleeding.

Each puppy should be followed by an afterbirth, which the dam will try to eat. Allow her to eat at least one as they contain important hormones affecting milk production. You must count the placentas to make absolutely sure that none was as retained in her; retained placentas can cause serious infection.

If the dam doesn't attend to the pup, dry the puppy and place it on the mother's nipple to nurse. You may have to help it by opening its mouth and squeezing a bit of milk into it. When the dam begins to strain to produce the next puppy, make sure she doesn't injure any pups she has already had. You can place the earlier born pups in a temporary box warmed to 90°F (32.2°C), but their removal may cause the dam to worry about them.

It is not always easy to tell when the last puppy is born. If you have any doubts, have your veterinarian check her (you should bring her and the pup-

The right match of puppy and owner is the recipe for a permanent, loving home.

pies for a postnatal check the next day anyway or, preferably, have a veterinarian who makes house calls check them). It is normal for the dam to have a dark greenish-black or purple vaginal discharge for several weeks after the birth, but any signs of infection or foul odor associated with it is cause for immediate concern.

Whelping Emergencies

You may have a whelping emergency if:

• more than 24 hours have passed since her temperature dropped without the onset of contractions
• more than two hours of intermittent contractions have passed without progressing to hard, forceful contractions.
• more than 30 minutes of strong contractions have passed without producing a puppy
• more than 15 minutes have passed since part of a puppy protruded through the vulva and the puppy makes no progress

- large amounts of blood are passed during whelping (the normal color fluid is dark green to black)

Never allow a dam in trouble to continue unaided. A Caesarean may be needed to save her life, and the longer it is put off, the poorer the chances of survival for her and her puppies will be.

Postnatal Care

Monitor the nursing puppies to make sure they are getting milk. Pups with cleft palates will have milk bubbling out of their nostrils as they attempt to nurse. Some pups must be helped onto the dam's nipples; some dam's nipples are too large to fit in a pup's mouth. You should weigh each puppy daily on a gram scale to make sure that it is gaining weight. If not, ask your veterinarian about supplemental feeding.

Puppies cannot regulate their body temperature, and chilling can quickly result in death. This is especially critical for smaller breeds. The dam is understandably reluctant to leave them at first, so you should place them in a warm box and encourage the dam to go out to relieve herself on a regular schedule. Never feed a chilled puppy, except for a few drops of sugar water. Maintain the pup's environment at 85 to 90°F (29.4–32.2°C) for the first week, 80°F (26.7°C) for the second week, and 75°F (23.9°C) for the third and fourth weeks. If you use a heating pad, cover it with a towel and make sure the pup can crawl away from it. Heat lamps have a tendency to overheat puppies, and should be avoided, or only used at a distance.

Sometimes one or more of the dam's breasts become hard, swollen, or painful, indicating mastitis. Warm compresses can help her feel more comfortable, but if pus and blood are mixed with the milk, you will need to prevent the pups from nursing from those nipples and your veterinarian will probably prescribe antibiotics, in which case you will have to feed the puppies by hand.

Eclampsia is a life-threatening convulsive condition that may occur in late pregnancy or, more commonly, during lactation. It is more prevalent in small breeds and with larger litters. The condition is brought about by a depletion of calcium. Many breeders of small dogs used to supplement with calcium throughout pregnancy in an attempt to ward off eclampsia, but it is now thought that such supplementation may actually promote eclampsia by interfering with the internal calcium-regulating mechanisms.

The first signs are nervous panting and restlessness, followed by increasing irritability and disorientation. Muscular twitching, fever, and rapid heart rate are definite danger signals. Convulsions are the last stage before death.

The bitch must be taken immediately to the veterinarian for an injection of calcium and Vitamin D in order to save her life. Calcium may be given by mouth if she can swallow and if the trip to the veterinarian is long, but even then may not help. Don't attempt to give oral medication if she is convulsing. *Eclampsia is an extreme emergency.*

In cases of infections, mastitis, or eclampsia you may have to wean the puppies early. By fitting the mother with a "body suit," such as a sweater sleeve with four leg holes, she can stay with the pups without letting them nurse.

Their Futures Are in Your Hands

The little lives before you now are there because of you. Remember that as you change the bedding for the fifth time that day, and later, mop the floor for the fiftieth. Puppies are a lot of work, but they are also a lot of fun. Their development is endlessly fascinating. Their tails are docked and dewclaws removed at about three days of age. The rule of thumb for docking JRT tails is to remove approximately one-third of the tail. This should leave about a 4 inch (10.2 cm) tail when grown—traditionally long enough to grab and use as a handle to pull a reluctant JRT out of a hole!

The puppies' eyes will open starting around ten days of age, and their ears around two weeks. This age marks the beginning of rapid mental and physical growth. They will attempt to walk at two weeks of age. Be sure to give them solid footing (*not* slippery newspaper).

Feeding: The dam will usually begin to wean her pups by four to six weeks of age; smaller pups may need to stay with her longer. At around three weeks, you can introduce the puppies to food—meat baby food or baby cereal or dry puppy food mixed with water and put through the blender is a good starter. They may lick it off your finger or you may have to put their noses in it. No matter what technique you use, be prepared to declare the feeding arena a major disaster area by the time the meal is over. Puppies seem to think they can best eat with their feet!

Socializing: After about six weeks of age, it is important that the puppies meet people so that they are well socialized, but this does not mean that they need to be exposed to a constant stream of new faces. Young puppies are irresistible, and your house may become the newest tourist attraction on the block. Don't let the puppies be handled by anyone outside of your family until the pups have had their vaccinations, and don't allow the mother to become stressed by onlookers. Talk to your veterinarian about your puppies' vaccination schedule and visitors, who could bring contagious diseases with them.

Placing the pups: There are two ways to place puppies: the ethical way and the unethical way. The unethical way is easy—sell each pup to the first comer for whatever you can get, and as soon as it leaves your house, wipe your hands of it. Don't think about the new owner who may not have a clue about raising a dog, not to mention a Jack Russell terrier. Don't think about the prospective buyer who is simply desperate for a Christmas present for the kids but really has no desire to keep it past the time they tire of it. Don't think about the uncaring person who wants a little money-maker that will be a puppy machine living in a cage until it dies of neglect. Yes, the unethical way is easy, until you try to sleep at night, every night for the next 12 years or so as you lay awake wondering what fate you sealed for the little being who trusted you to care about its future.

The ethical way is initially more difficult, but will be easier if you have quality puppies with which to attract quality homes. If you have a worthy breeding, word of mouth within the JRT world will be your best advertisement, but you can supplement with ads in dog magazines, and in various newspapers. You must play detective in ascertaining if prospective buyers have the sort of home in which you would be comfortable placing a puppy. Once a sale has been made, the ethical breeder maintains contact with the puppy owner, and finally, the ethical breeder agrees that no matter what the age and what the reason, if the new owner can no longer keep the dog, it is always welcome back at its birthplace. The smart ethical breeder spells out these terms in a written contract. If you can't make the commitment to be an ethical breeder, please don't be a breeder at all.

It may take time, but you can find a good home. Of course, after a while it may become obvious that the good home you find is your own!

Jack of All Trades

For a Jack Russell terrier, work and play are synonymous. An outing in the field spent in search of quarry, whether real or just dreamed of, is enough to make any JRT's day complete. For their owners, often justifiably smitten with a case of "my dog is better than your dog," there are a host of competitions in which to prove their dog's mettle. Jack Russell terriers will merrily agree to participate in just about anything you consider fun, without regard to whether any ribbons or trophies are involved.

A Walk on the Wild Side

JRTs can entertain themselves quite ably within the confines of your own yard, but some of that entertainment may include digging up your garden, ripping down hanging clothes, and gnawing on your house. Regular exer-

A walk involves checking out every nook and cranny along the way.

cise will lessen this misdirected energy considerably.

JRTs are equally adept at finding trouble afield. You will find your visions of a faithful dog trotting by your side at odds with the JRT's instinctive urge to root out some vermin. Bringing along another reliable dog that stays with you is the best training aid you can have; otherwise, staying in an area with defined paths and walking along them at a brisk pace seems to work better than simply standing in the middle of a field or the woods. The chance of your dog wandering off to hunt is less if you avoid thick wooded areas or any areas chock full of game. Even squirrels can be a problem if there are so many that once one has been chased up a tree, there is always another just a little bit further away beckoning to be chased as well. JRTs won't hesitate to give chase to any size game, and it is your responsibility to know your running area thoroughly before ever removing your JRT's leash. Is there a road around the bend in a path? A fast-running canal? A cliff? Alligators? Porcupines? Mineshafts? Caves? Burrows? Thin ice? Explore an area with your JRT on a long lead several times before trusting it off lead.

If you want to trust your JRT, trust it first in an enclosed area such as a fenced ball field or empty schoolyard. Bring some treats so you can practice off-lead recalls. You may even want to make sure that your dog is already hungry (and maybe a little tired) beforehand. When your dog comes, praise it, hand it a treat, then let it go again so it doesn't associate coming with relinquishing its freedom.

When your dog is returning to you reliably in a fenced area, you may wish to venture farther afield. Note that walking a JRT off lead entails some risk, which you should carefully consider before you unsnap the leash. One of the deadliest killers of JRTs is trust. The JRT is not a retriever that can be trusted to walk off lead by your side down a country road, or to sit in your unfenced front yard. As trustworthy as your JRT may be, it can't help but follow its instinct to answer the call of the wild and to chase game, and far too often it's off like a bolt after a cat in the distance, across the path of an oncoming vehicle. Trust is wonderful, but careless or blind trust is deadly.

In many areas there simply are no safe places in which to run your terrier off lead. Your dog can get ample exercise and enjoyment from a walk on lead. Before walking on lead, double check that your dog's collar cannot slip over its head. A startled dog can frantically back out of its collar unless it is snug. Once it learns this little trick, it won't hesitate to employ it to get a closer look at the neighbor's cats along the route. If you use a retractable leash, never allow so much loose lead that your dog could suddenly jump in the path of a passing vehicle. Be prepared for the typical Jack Russell jackrabbit starts and jackknife turns.

If you pick a regular time of day for your walk, you will have your own personal fitness coach goading you off the couch like clockwork. Check your dog's footpads regularly for signs of abrasion, foreign bodies, tears, or blistering from hot pavement. Leave your dog at home in hot weather. Dogs are unable to cool themselves through sweating, and heatstroke in jogging dogs is a common emergency seen by veterinarians in the summer. In winter, check between the pads for balls of ice (coating the paws with Vaseline can help keep the ice balls down some-

They can even retrieve—but they may not give up the stick once they reach you!

what), and rinse the feet when returning from walking on rock salt.

Swimming is an excellent exercise, especially in the summer or for dogs with arthritis or other injuries. Most JRTs take right to the water, but if you have one that needs a little coaxing, get right in the water with it and ease it in gradually. Support its rear end so that it doesn't splash on top of the water, and you will soon have a JRT sea otter on your hands.

Some JRT owners encourage their dogs to follow their instincts and hunt. Barns may harbor a bevy of rats that your terrier may be able to seek and destroy. Always beware that many holes that attract small mammals also attract snakes, some of which may be poisonous. Rat bites, too, can pose a danger. If your heart is set on hunting larger game, be aware that in the United States it is illegal to hunt fur-bearing animals in their dens. Most JRT owners find that terrier trials are the best way to satisfy their terrier's love of the hunt.

Rats! Layout for go-to-ground competition.

They're off! Jack Russell terrier racing is the most popular and exciting of JRT competitions.

A favorite backyard game, as well as good practice for racing, is a lure hung from a pole and dragged around erratically. Make sure your neighbors aren't at home!

Trials and Tribulations

Perhaps because JRTs think just about anything that involves movement is great fun, the list of organized activities available to them is extensive. JRTCA- and JRTBA-sponsored competitions include go-to-ground, racing, conformation, obedience, agility, trailing and locating, high jump, and water races.

Go-to-ground competitions are traditionally the most important of the competitions. In these trials, terriers must enter a man-made but natural-appearing tunnel, at the end of which are caged animals (usually rats). Dogs are expected to enter the hole without hesitation, traverse the tunnel, and work the quarry by barking, digging, growling, and whining.

The JRTCA awards several levels of certificates for go-to-ground performances: the Sporting Certificate, the Trial Certificate, and the most prestigious Natural Hunting Certificate Below Ground in the Field. Those that earn Natural Hunting certificates for three different types of quarry are honored with the JRTCA Bronze Working Terrier Medallion for Special Merit in the Field.

Terrier trials are also sponsored by the American Working Terrier Association. The Novice class consists of a 10-foot-long (3.1 m) tunnel with one turn. The dog is released 10 feet from the tunnel entrance, and is given one minute to traverse the tunnel and begin working the caged rats. Working should continue for 30 seconds, after which the dog is lifted out of a trapdoor. The handler can help direct the dog to the entrance and encourage it to work the rat, but such help will result in a nonqualifying score. Still, since most people don't have access to trenches and rats in their backyard, it is not uncommon to use the first trial as a training exercise; but the next trial your terrier will be ready! Training runs are also held after the end of most trials, using wooden above-ground tunnels. Open classes consist of 30-foot-long (9.1 m) tunnels with three turns. Dogs have 30 seconds to reach the quarry, and must work it for one minute. Qualifiers are awarded the Certificate of Gameness.

Racing is the most popular and spectacular of JRT competitions. Sanctioned trials may either be run on a flat track or over four to six low hurdles, over a distance of 150 to 240 feet (45.7–73.2 m). The track is about 6 to 8 feet (1.8–2.4 m) wide and fenced, with a catch area behind the finish. Dogs are divided according to height (over and under 12½ inches [31.8 cm]). Six dogs may compete in a single race. All sanctioned trials require that dogs run muzzled.

To test your JRTs enthusiasm, hang a lure (pelt, fake fur, or even old sock) from a short pole and "tease" your dog by dragging the lure away from it. Let the dog catch the lure occasionally, and quit before your JRT is tired. Next, teach your JRT to play the game while wearing a muzzle, and to pay attention to the lure when placed in a starting box.

Also practice running the lure through a JRT-size hole between some hay bales. At races, the winner is determined according to which dog runs through the hay bale bottleneck first. The final step is running with other terriers, and if you have done your homework, your JRT is very likely to ignore its competitors and chase the lure with single-minded intent. In fairness to the other competitors, don't run your JRT if you have any doubts about its ability to "run clean."

Conformation competition is similar to that at any dog show, with each dog evaluated in comparison to the standard of perfection. Type and soundness, with an emphasis on the structure necessary to do the job of a working JRT, are paramount. Dogs should be trained to trot smartly

Ahhh, the good life. JRTs have been known to relax.

beside you on lead, and to stand at attention, with legs parallel to each other and front legs and rear hocks perpendicular to the ground. Discreet use of a squeaky toy or piece of fur is helpful in focusing the dog's attention and keeping it happy in the ring.

Obedience trial requirements may vary from trial to trial, but are generally not unlike AKC trials. Sub-Novice exercises are all on lead and include heeling, heeling in a figure eight, stand for exam, recall, one minute sit/stay, and three minute down/stay (stays are judged in a group); Novice exercises are the same but include off-lead heeling, recall, and stays. Open exercises include more advanced exercises and require retrieving and jumping. Utility requires scent discrimination, and directed retrieving and jumping. Exercises are scored and in order to earn an obedience certificate a terrier must score 170 out of 200 possible points (and at least 50 percent for each exercise) on three separate occasions.

Agility competition requires a combination of obedience and athleticism, all of which adds up to a lot of fun and excitement! Dogs traverse tunnels, ramps, and hurdles, with various levels

An excited spectator roots on his favorite.

They're off!

of difficulty. More advanced classes are off lead, but on-lead competitions are available for beginners. Agility certificates are awarded for three qualifying scores. Agility classes for all breeds are springing up in larger cities throughout the country, and you may be able to find a group in your area. If not, you can improvise your own set of obstacles in your backyard (as long as you don't care what the neighbors think).

Trailing and locating competition requires dogs to follow a scent through a short tunnel and an open area to locate a simulated quarry. Start with very short trails, gradually working backwards, further from the quarry. JRTs are natural sniffers, and most catch on quickly as long as it leads to fun. Incidentally, if your JRT is adept at this, and you want to provide a real service to the community, you might consider search-and-rescue training, where dogs use their noses (and other senses) to find lost people or bodies. The ever ready and versatile JRT is a natural at this most rewarding endeavor.

The Jack Russell terrier has proven time and again that it is a dog for all reasons. But no one can deny that the most fun with JRTs comes with snuggling in front of a fire on a winter evening, hiking through the woods on an autumn day, squirrel watching on a summer morning, and sharing a picnic lunch on a spring afternoon—and luckily, no one has yet devised a competi-

Traversing the A-frame in an agility course.

tion for them. For owners young and old, from inquisitive pup to active adult to loyal senior citizen, for companionship and competition, the Jack Russell terrier is not only a jack of all trades—it's master of all!

Useful Addresses and Literature

Organizations
(Note that addresses may change.)

The Jack Russell Terrier Club of
    America, Inc.
    P.O. Box 4527
    Lutherville, MD 21094-4527
    (410) 561-3655

The Jack Russell Terrier
    Breeder's Association
    P.O. Box 115
    Winchester Center, CT 06094
    (203) 379-3282

The Jack Russell Terrier Club of
    Canada
    Yvonne Downey
    242 Henrietta Street
    Fort Erie, Ontario
    Canada, L2A 2K7
    (905) 871-8691

The Jack Russell Terrier Club of
    Great Britain
    Chairperson: Greg Mousley
    Aston Heath Farm
    Sudbury, Derbyshire
    England DEGS88

The American Working Terrier
    Association
    Frank Doing, Corresponding
    Secretary
    P.O. Box QQ
    East Quogue, NY 11942

Russell Rescue (JRTCA)
    Caherine Romaine Brown
    4757 Lakeville Road
    Geneseo, NY 14454-9731
    (716) 243-0929

Orthopedic Foundation for Animals
    (OFA)
    2300 Nifong Boulevard
    Columbia, MO 65201
    (314) 442-0418

Canine Eye Registration
    Foundation (CERF)
    South Campus Courts C
    Purdue University
    West Lafayette, IN 47906

Home Again Microchip Service
    1-800-LONELY-ONE

Magazines
True Grit
    Official publication of the JRTCA

Parson's Nook
    Official publication of the JRTBA

Down to Earth
    Official publication of the AWTA

Dog Fancy
    PO Box 53264
    Boulder, CO 80322-3264
    (303) 666-8504

Dogs USA Annual
    P.O. Box 55811
    Boulder, CO 80322-5811
    (303) 786-7652

Dog World
29 North Wacker Drive
Chicago, IL 60606-3298
(312) 726-2802

Books

Atter, Sheila. *Jack Russell Terriers Today.* Glousestershire, Great Britain: Ringpress Books, Ltd. 1995.

Chapman, Eddie. *The Working Jack Russell Terrier.* Dorchester, Great Britain: Henry King at the Dorset Press, 1985.

Jackson, Jean and Frank. *The Making of the Parson Jack Russell Terrier.* Dover, New Hampshire: The Boydell Press, 1986.

Jackson, Jean and Frank. *Parson Jack Russell Terriers: An Owner's Companion.* Great Britain: The Crowood Press, 1990.

Jackson, Jean and Frank. *The Parson and Jack Russell Terriers.* London: Popular Dogs Publishing Co, Ltd., 1991.

Lent, Patricia. *Sport With Terriers.* Rome, New York: Arner Publications, 1973.

Index

Grades of dogs, 22
Grooming, 62–68
Guests, interaction with, 41
Gums, 27

Harness, 31
Head, 15
 wounds, 73
Health, 12–14
 care, 69–82
 emergencies, 70–71
Hearing, sense of, 53
Heart disease, 77
Heartworms, 75
Heat, 19, 85–86
 stroke, 72
"Heel" command, 56–57
Hepatitis, 76
Hindquarters, 16
Hock, 14
Hookworms, 75
Housebreaking, 38–39
Hyperactivity, 39–40
Hyperadrenocorticism, 78
Hypoglycemia, 73
Hypothermia, 72
Hypothyroidism, 78

Immune system, 80
Impetigo, 64
Independence, 11
Insect:
 growth regulators, 65–66
 stings, 73
Intelligence, 11
Intestinal parasites, 75

Jack Russell Terrier Breeder's
 Association, 9, 98
 registration, 20
Jack Russell Terrier Club of
 America, 9, 98
 breed standard, 15–18
 registration, 18, 20
Jack Russell Terrier Club of
 Canada, 98
Jack Russell Terrier Club of
 Great Britain, 9, 98
Jack Russell Terriers Today,
 99

Jackson, Jean and Frank, 99
Jumping up, 34

KCS, 79
Kennel cough, 77
Keratoconjunctivitis, 79
Kidney disease, 78
Knee injuries, 79–80
Knuckles, 27

Labor, 87–88
Leash, 31
Leg length, 20
Legg-Calve-Perthes disease, 13
Legs, straightness, 27
Lens luxation, 12–13, 79
Lent, Patricia, 99
Leptospirosis, 76
Level bite, 14
License tags, 46–47
Limping, 79–80
Locating, 97
Loin, 14
Long legged, 20
Lungworms, 75
Lyme disease, 64

*Making of the Parson Jack
 Russell Terrier, The,* 99
Malathion, flea control, 65
Male reproductive organs, 87
Medication, administering, 74
Mineral supplements, 61
Mouth, 16
 to nose resuscitation, 72

Nails, 66–67
 clippers, 31
Neck, 16
Nervousness, 51–52
Neutering, 19
Newspaper ads, 23
Nose pigmentation, 26
Nutrition, 58–61
 fat, 60
 feeding schedules, 60
 food types, 58
 nutrient levels, 58–59
 obesity, 61
 protein, 59–60

Obedience, 95
Obesity, 60–61
Occiput, 14
Occlusion problems, 13
Odors, 68, 80
Olfaction, 52
Open wounds, 73
Organic flea control, 65
Orthopedic Foundation for
 Animals, 98
Osteoarthritis, 80
Owner considerations, 19–27
 age, 19
 breeders, 22
 coat, 20
 gender, 19–20
 grade, 22
 leg length, 20
 quality, 21
 quantity, 20–21
 registration, 20
 sources, 22–25

Pain, sense of, 53, 56
Panting, 51
Parainfluenza, 76
Parasites, internal, 75–76
*Parson and Jack Russell
 Terriers, The,* 99
Parson Jack Russell Terrier
 Club, 9
*Parson Jack Russell Terriers: An
 Owner's Companion,* 99
Parson's Nook, 98
Parvovirus, 76
Patellar luxation, 13
Pedigree, four generation, 18
Pen, exercise, 31–32
Permethrin, flea control, 65
Pesticides, natural, 65
Pet:
 quality, 22
 shops, 23
Plants, poisonous, 30
Plaque, 67
Poisoning, 30, 71
Poop scoop, 31, 33
Postnatal care 90
Pregnancy, 86–87
 false, 86